gage Cornerstones

CANADIAN LANGUAGE ARTS

Anthology 5a

gage EDUCATIONAL PUBLISHING COMPANY
A DIVISION OF CANADA PUBLISHING CORPORATION
Vancouver · Calgary · Toronto · London · Halifax

Permission Editor: Elizabeth Long

Researchers: Todd Mercer, Monika Croydon, Monica Kulling

Bias Consultant: Margaret Hoogeveen

Cover Illustration: Daphne McCormack

Acknowledgments

Every reasonable effort has been made to trace ownership of copyrighted material. Information that would enable the publisher to correct any reference or credit in future editions would be appreciated.

7 "Steel Band Jump Up" © 1994 by Faustin Charles from *A Caribbean Dozen* edited by John Agard & Grace Nichols. By permission of the publisher Walker Books Ltd., London. Published in the U.S. by Candlewick Press, Cambridge, MA. / 8-11 "Greetings Everyone" from *Greetings!* by Karin Luisa Badt. By permission of Children's Press Inc., a Grolier Publishing Company, © 1994. / 14 "Hey World, Here I Am!" from *Hey World, Here I Am!* by Jean Little used by permission of Kids Can Press Ltd., Toronto. © 1986 by Jean Little. / 16-23 "Grandpa Chatterji" excerpted from *Grandpa Chatterji* by Jamila Gavin. By permission of Methuen Children's Books Ltd. © 1993. / 26-31 "Dawa and Olana: Boys of Mongolia" from *Mongolia: Vanishing Cultures* © 1994 by Jan Reynolds, reproduced by permission of Harcourt Brace & Company. / 36-41 *The Day of Ahmed's Secret* by Florence Parry Heide and Judith Heide Gilliland. Text © 1990 by Florence Parry Heide and Judith Heide Gilliland. Illustration © 1990 by Ted Lewin. By permission of Lothrop, Lee & Shepard Books, a division of William Morrow & Company Inc. / 44-49 "Out of the Dump" from *Out of the Dump: Writings and Photographs by Children from Guatemala*. Edited by Kristine L. Franklin & Nancy McGirr. Translated from the Spanish by Kristine L. Franklin. Text © 1995 by Kristine L. Franklin. Photos © 1995 by Out of the Dump: Photographs by Children from Guatemala City's Garbage Dump. By permission of Lothrop, Lee & Shepard Books, a division of William Morrow & Company Inc. / 53 "Enjoy the Earth" from *Earthways, Earthwise* by Judith Nicholls © 1993. By permission of Oxford University Press. / 54-57 "Going Buggy in the Trees" by Faron Nicholas and Douglas Cowell from *Wild Magazine* (February 1996), Vol. 1, No. 5. Reprinted with permission of the authors. / 60 "Poem for the Ancient Trees" by Robert Priest from *Images of Nature* compiled by David Booth. By permission of the author. / 62-64 "Apes on the Go" adapted from *Real Live Science* by Jay Ingram © 1992. By permission of the publisher, Greey de Pencier Books Inc., Toronto, Canada. / 66 "Think of the Ocean..." by Siobhan Swayne from *Here is a Poem* published by the League of Canadian Poets © 1983. / 68-73 "Atlantic Seashore", excerpt from *At the Seashore* by Pamela Hickman. By permission of Formac Publishing Company Ltd. Text © 1996 by Pamela Hickman. Illustrations by Twila Robar-DeCoste. / 78-81 Excerpts from *Above the Treeline* by Anne Cooper. Illustrated by Dorothy Emerling. Part of the Wild Wonders Series © 1996. By permission of Denver Museum of Natural History. / 84-91 "Garbage Creek" from *Garbage Creek and Other Stories* © 1997 by W.D. Valgardson. A Groundwood Book/Douglas & McIntyre. / 94 "The Web of Life" from *Spirit Walker* by Nancy Wood © 1993 by Nancy Wood. By permission of Bantam Doubleday Dell Books for Young Readers. / 97 "A Song of Greatness" translated by Mary Austin from *The Children Sing in the Far West* by Mary Austin. © 1928 by Mary Austin. © renewed 1956 by Kenneth M. Chapman and Mary C. Wheelwright. Reprinted by permission of Houghton Mifflin Company. / 100-105 Excerpt from *Super Heroes* by Claire Watts and Robert Nicholson. By permission of Two-Can Publishing © 1994. / 108-113 "Bellerophon and the Flying Horse" from

Canadian Cataloguing in Publication Data

Main entry under title:

Gage cornerstones: Canadian language arts. Anthology, 5a

ISBN 0-7715-1208-2

1. Readers (Elementary).   I. McClymont, Christine.
II. Title: Cornerstones Canadian language arts.
III. Title: Anthology, 5a

PE1121.G25 1998   428.6   C98-930973-8

Tales From Ancient Greece retold by Pamela Oldfield, illustrated by Nick Harris, published by Kingfisher Books. © 1988 by Grisewood & Dempsey Ltd. / 116-119 "The Search for the Magic Lake" from *Wonder Tales from Around the World* by Heather Forest (August House, 1995). © 1995 by Heather Forest. Reprinted by permission. / 122 "Brave New Heights" by Monica Kulling. © 1998 by Monica Kulling. Reprinted by permission of Marian Reiner for the author. / 124 "Harriet Tubman" by Eloise Greenfield from *Pass It On: African-American Poetry for Children* selected by Wade Hudson. © 1993 by Wade Hudson 126-131 "The Wreck of the Dispatch" by Janet Lunn from *Larger Than Life*. Reprinted with permission of the author © 1979. / 134-135 "Dwaina Brooks: Feeding the Homeless" from *Amazing Kids!* by Paula N. Kessler. © 1995 by RGA Publishing Group, Inc. Reprinted by permission of Random House, Inc. / 138-141 "The First of Many Steps" from *Super Kids: Young Heroes in Action* by Leslie Garrett. © 1997 by Leslie Garrett. Published by Harper Collins Publishers Ltd. Reprinted by permission of Harper Collins Publishers Ltd. 145 Covers reprinted with permission of *Owl, Cricket, New Moon, Sports Illustrated for Kids, Yes Mag,* and *Kidsworld Magazine.* 154-157 *Wild* covers reprinted with permission.

Photo Credits

8 left Orion Press/Tony Stone Images; **8 right** UN/DPI 146122 D. Monsen; **9** Eric Sandford/Tom Stack & Associates; **10 top** Charles Gupton/Tony Stone Images; **10 bottom** Corbis-Bettmann; **11 top** Robert Frerck/Odyssey; **11 bottom** Martin R. Jones/Unicorn Stock Photos; **54** Douglas Cowell; **55 bottom left, right** Christian Autotte; **56** Douglas Cowell; **57 top** Douglas Cowell; **57 bottom left, right** Christian Autotte; **63 left** Allen Altcheck, OFI; **63 middle** Wendy Hoole, OFI; **63 right** Alan Shildo; **68-69** J.A. Kraulis/Masterfile; **76** David Hines Studio, Wolfville, NS; **77** Suzanne Hobin; **103 top** Corbis/Everett; **103 bottom** Everett Collection; **107 top, bottom** Everett Collection; **114** Dave Starrett; **120 left** Macchu Picchu/Valan Photos; **120 right** Corel; **121** Hulton Getty/Tony Stone Images; **124** Massachusetts Historical Society, Boston, Mass.; Grey Villet for LIFE; **132** Alan Wilkinson; **133** Pronk&Associates; **137 left** G. Kopelow/First Light; **137 right** Valan Photos; **140, 141** Sam McLeod/London Free Press; **143 left, right** Valan Photos; **144 bottom right** Corel; **154 top left, middle, top right** Martin McLennan; **155 bottom** Dave Denning; **156-157 top middle** Pronk&Associates; **157 bottom right** Martin McLennan; **158 top** David C. Fritz; **158 bottom** Henry H. Holdsworth; **159 left** Rich Kirchner; **159 right** Kennan Ward.

Illustrations

12-13 Dan Hobbs; **25** Joe Weissman; **32-33** Barbara Spurll; **43** Jack McMaster; **52-53** Farida Zaman; **59** Steve Attoe; **67, 74-75 bottom** Margaret Hathaway; **74 top** David Marshak; **96-97** Martin Springett; **100-101** Phil Gascoine; **102** Corbis-Bettmann Archive; **104** Corel; **105** Charles Fiddler; **115** Bill Suddick

ISBN 0-7715-**1208**-2
2 3 4 5 6 BP 04 03 02 01 00 99
Printed and bound in Canada.

Cornerstones Development Team

HERE ARE THE PEOPLE WHO WORKED HARD TO MAKE THIS BOOK EXCITING FOR YOU!

WRITING TEAM
Christine McClymont
Patrick Lashmar
Dennis Strauss
Patricia FitzGerald-Chesterman
Cam Colville
Robert Cutting
Stephen Hurley
Luigi Iannacci
Oksana Kuryliw
Caroline Lutyk

GAGE EDITORIAL
Joe Banel
Rivka Cranley
Elizabeth Long
David MacDonald
Evelyn Maksimovich
Diane Robitaille
Darleen Rotozinski
Jennifer Stokes
Carol Waldock

GAGE PRODUCTION
Anna Kress
Bev Crann

DESIGN, ART DIRECTION & ELECTRONIC ASSEMBLY
Pronk&Associates

ADVISORY TEAM
Connie Fehr Burnaby SD, BC
Elizabeth Sparks Delta SD, BC
John Harrison Burnaby SD, BC
Joan Alexander St. Albert PSSD, AB
Carol Germyn Calgary B of E, AB
Cathy Sitko Edmonton Catholic SD, AB
Laura Haight Saskatoon SD, SK
Linda Nosbush Prince Albert SD, SK
Linda Tysowski Saskatoon PSD, SK
Maureen Rodniski Winnipeg SD, MB
Cathy Saytar Dufferin-Peel CDSB, ON
Jan Adams Thames Valley DSB, ON
Linda Ross Thames Valley DSB, ON
John Cassano York Region DSB, ON
Carollynn Desjardins Nipissing-Parry Sound CDSB, ON
David Hodgkinson Waterloo Region DSB, ON
Michelle Longlade Halton CDSB, ON
Sharon Morris Toronto CDSB, ON
Ann Louise Revalls Ottawa-Carleton CSB, ON
Heather Sheehan Toronto CDSB, ON
Ruth Scott Brock University, ON
Elizabeth Thorn Nipissing University, ON
Jane Abernethy Chipman & Fredericton SD, NB
Darlene Whitehouse-Sheehan Chipman & Fredericton SD, NB
Carol Chandler Halifax Regional SB, NS
Martin MacDonald Strait Regional Board, NS
Ray Doiron University of PEI, PE
Robert Dawe Avalon East SD, NF
Margaret Ryall Avalon East SD, NF

Contents

4

SOCIAL STUDIES FOCUS

Heroes Old and New

GENRE STUDY

Make a Magazine

Poem by
Faustin Charles

Picture by
Kim LaFave

Steel Band Jump Up

I put my ear to the ground,
And I hear the steel band sound:
Ping pong! Ping pong!
Music deep, rhythm sweet,
I'm dancing tracking the beat;
Like a seashell's ringing song,
Ping pong! Ping pong!
Moving along, moving along,
High and low, up and down,
Ping pong! Ping pong!
Pan beating singing, round and round,
Ping pong! Ping pong!

7

Greetings, Everyone!

Article by **Karin Luisa Badt**

Hello! *Bom dia! Ming-gah-bou! Shalom! Ni-hao-ma!* If you're walking down the street and you see a friend, you probably wave, or smile, or say "Hi." Maybe you do all three!

Japan

Kenya

Waving
Waving is a common greeting in many parts of the world, probably because it is one of the most visible ways to catch people's attention when you spot them at a distance.

8

Hello

The phrases below are greetings in these languages:

Bom dia, Portuguese

Ming-gah-bou, Ga, a language spoken in Ghana

Shalom, Hebrew

Ni-hao-ma, Mandarin

These are all ways of *greeting* your friend. Greetings are things that people say or do to show that they recognize the presence of another person. Every culture in the world uses them.

Greetings may be quite simple—like smiling or shaking hands—but they are very important. By greeting one another, people confirm that they have some kind of relationship. If they had no relationship, they would just ignore each other!

Greetings are also important because almost every human interaction begins with one. Usually, people do not just start talking to each other; first they greet one another, and then they begin talking.

When school begins, your teacher probably says something like "Good morning, class." He or she doesn't just say "Open your math books!"

But does everyone throughout the world greet each other the same way? The answer is no.

Every culture has its own rules about how to greet people—what to say and do. Even in the same culture, the rules can differ according to the people and the situation.

People follow their culture's greeting rules without even thinking about it. Do you say "Good morning" to neighbours you see on your way to school? If you do, it's because in your culture, this is the polite way to greet a neighbour in the morning. You probably *wouldn't* say "Yabba-dabba-doo!"

Greetings are more than just words. Body language—the way you stand, the look on your face, the movements you make—also plays a large role. And the way people use their bodies when they greet each other varies from culture to culture. Do people bow their heads or shake hands? Do they come close to the other person or stay far away? In some countries people actually touch the other person, while in others, this would be considered impolite.

Little leaguers

Bedouin men stroke their beards when they meet someone. The Polynesians of Tahiti rub noses. Japanese people bow; the more important the person being greeted, the lower the bow.

In many countries, friends kiss each other on the cheeks every time they meet. The number of kisses depends on the country. In Mexico, you give a friend just one kiss on the cheek. In Egypt, people kiss three times: first on one cheek, then on the other, and then back to the first cheek. And if you ever go to Italy, get ready to pucker up. People there kiss each other *four* times—twice on each cheek!

Japanese businesspeople
In Japan, it is the custom to bow when greeting someone. An *eshaku* (a slight bow) is for friends and business associates. A *futusurei* (a medium bow) is for people with whom you are not as close. And a *saikeirei* (a deep bow, almost to the floor) is used when meeting extremely important people. It is not used much.

Maori women, New Zealand
Pressing noses together, a custom called *hongi,* is the traditional way Maori people greet each other.

People sometimes use special greetings to show that they have something in common, such as their age. In Canada and the United States, children and teenagers often exchange "high-fives" when they meet. In Hungary, teenagers kiss each other's cheeks three times.

Shaking hands, like kissing, is popular throughout the world. In some places, like Germany, friends usually greet each other with a handshake. In other places, like Canada and the United States, handshakes tend to be used mainly when meeting someone for the first time, or in a business situation, such as a job interview.

The handshake has been with us for thousands of years. Originally, men shook hands with each other to show that they were not carrying weapons.

FOLLOW UP

Which greetings did you find the most interesting? Which photos surprised you? Do you know how people greet each other in any other countries?

Understanding the Article

"Yabba-dabba-doo!"

- Why are greetings important to people?

- What does "body language" mean? Find four examples of greetings using body language.

- What are some special greetings you and your friends use?

"HELLO" AROUND THE WORLD

Friendly Greeting	Language
merhaba	Turkish
sakubona	Zulu
swa-dee-ka	Thai (for female friends)
swa-dee-kup	(for male friends)

"Hello" in Many Languages

The article tells you how to say "hello" in several languages. Find out how to say "hello" in other languages—perhaps the language you speak at home! Make a big class chart called *"Hello" Around the World.* See the chart at left for a few new examples to get you started.

Act It Out!

We all use body language to communicate our feelings. Body language includes the expressions on our faces, the way we stand, movements, and gestures. Work with a partner. Try acting angry, excited, happy, peaceful, sad, or afraid. See if your partner can guess the emotion you are expressing.

Mini Travel Guide

If you travel to another country, you'll probably want to learn the customs of the people who live there. That way, you'll feel more comfortable and they'll see that you respect their ways.

Pick a country that you would like to visit. Research to find out about the local customs (for example: how people greet each other, what they eat, where they shop, how they say **goodbye** or **thank you**). Travel guidebooks are good sources of information, or you could interview someone you know who has been to that country. Then write your own mini travel guide for people who would also like to visit this country.

 TECH LINK
If you can use multimedia software, you could develop a computer-based presentation.

Look It Up!

Do you know what the following words mean?

culture

custom

gesture

interaction

relationship

symbolic

traditional

Write a definition for each of these words in your notebooks. If you're not sure of the meaning, use a dictionary.

Hey World, Here I Am!

Poem by **Jean Little**

I said to the world, "I've arrived.
I, Kate Bloomfield, have come at last."
The World paid no attention.
I said to the World, "Hey World, here I am!
Don't you understand?
It's me, Kate Bloomfield."
The World ignored me.
I took myself off into a corner.
"Guess what?" I whispered. "I made it.
You know...Kate Bloomfield."
My Self bellowed, "YeaaaAAY, Kate!"
And spun six somersaults up the middle of Main Street.
The World turned.
"What did you say?" said the World.
I paid no attention.
After all, I gave it its chance.
It's not my fault that it missed me.

Pictures by **Louise Phillips**

Class Discussion

You've just read two poems about kids and the way they see the world. Discuss with your classmates

- Which of the poems was more fun to read? Why?

- Which kid wants to take on the world and win?

- Which kid wants to learn all about the world?

- Which kid has more positive feelings about him or herself?

Nothing Else

Poem by Kit Wright

There's nothing I can't see
From here.

There's nothing I can't be
From here.

Because my eyes
Are open wide
To let the big
World come inside,

I think I can see me
From here.

A Poem

You, too, are a kid getting ready to take on the world. Do you think of the world as large or small? Friendly or challenging? What message would you like to send to the world?

First, think about messages you could send, and then write all your ideas down quickly. Next, choose the ideas you like the best and shape them into a poem. You may choose either poem as a model, or create your own form.

Neetu and Sanjay live in England. They have just learned that their Grandpa Chatterji is coming to visit them, all the way from India. They have never met him. How do you think they feel?

Story by
Jamila Gavin

Pictures by
Joe Weissmann

Grandpa Chatterji

Neetu and her little brother Sanjay have two grandpas—Mom's dad and Dad's dad.

Mom's dad lives in India and they have never ever seen him. But Dad's dad lives in Leicester and they see him quite often.

Although they love and respect Dad's dad, as head of the family, Neetu and Sanjay are a little afraid of him. Whenever he comes to visit, they all have to be on their toes.

If Neetu wears jeans, Grandpa Leicester frowns at her and snorts, "I don't like my granddaughter wearing jeans," so she has to go and put on a dress. If Sanjay, who is a terrible chatterbox, sometimes interrupts, Grandfather glares at him sternly and says, "I don't like little boys who interrupt," and Sanjay has to bite his lip and try so hard not to speak.

When their mother got a job and went out to work, Grandfather was very disapproving. "I don't like my daughter-in-law going out to work." Mom just smiled politely, and went anyway, and Dad took his father aside to try to explain how with Mom going to work, they could afford a new car.

Perhaps the worst time is when Dad's dad comes to stay and they can't eat their favourite pizza and chips. Instead, they have to eat vegetable curry, runny spinach with eggs, and other stuff they think is horrible.

✹ ✹ ✹

One day, Mom said excitedly, "Children! Your grandpa is coming to stay! Isn't that wonderful!" But they didn't think it was wonderful at all. Neetu just groaned and said, "Oh no! I'll have to wear nothing but dresses," and Sanjay moaned, "Oh no! We'll have to eat curried eggs."

It was Dad who beamed at them and said, "It's not my dad from Leicester who's coming to visit us, it's your Mom's dad from Calcutta. You've never met him! You can call him 'Grandpa Chatterji.'"

Neetu and Sanjay looked at each other doubtfully. How could they know whether a grandad from Calcutta was any different from a grandad from Leicester, even if he was called Grandpa Chatterji? They would just have to wait and see.

All that week Mom went round with a smile on her face, and even Dad seemed quite relaxed. Mom got the spare room ready, just as she always did for Dad's dad. But instead of worriedly scrubbing and cleaning and polishing and checking that there was not one speck of dust to be seen anywhere in the house, she actually hummed and sang and seemed to enjoy making everything look nice.

✹ ✹ ✹

On the day of his arrival, Mom and Dad got up very early and drove off to the airport to meet Grandpa Chatterji. Neetu and Sanjay didn't go because there wouldn't be room in the car on the way back. Mrs. Bennet from next door came in to look after them.

They waited and waited. Sanjay looked out of one window and Neetu looked out of the other. What would he be like? Would he wear a smart suit and shiny black shoes like Dad's dad? Would he smoke cigars and sit in the best easy chair and talk business with Dad in a big boomy voice? Would he be served first at the table? Would he always insist on using the bathroom first in the morning, even though he took the longest and made them late for school? And would he be critical and strict and insist on total obedience at all times?

They waited and waited. Suddenly, Sanjay shouted, "They're here!" The little red Mini had pulled up outside the house.

"Oh dear," cried Neetu, suddenly going all shy, "I'm going to hide."

They both hid behind the sofa. They heard the front door open. They heard Mom come in and say gently, "Welcome to our home!" They heard Dad say, "I'll take your luggage up to your room," and they heard a thin, quiet, soft voice say, "And where are my little grandchildren?"

Then there was silence. Crouched behind the sofa, Neetu and Sanjay hardly breathed. Then suddenly, although they didn't hear Grandpa Chatterji come into the room, they knew he was there because they saw a pair of bare, dark-brown, knobbly, long-toed bony feet.

The feet came and stood right close by them. The feet emerged from beneath thin, white trousers, and as their eyes travelled all the way up, past a white tunic and brown waistcoat and past a red and blue woolly scarf round the neck, they found themselves looking into a round, shining, kind, wrinkly face, with deep-as-oceans large, brown eyes, and a mass of pure, white, fluffy hair which fell in a tangle over his brow.

"Ah!" exclaimed Grandpa Chatterji with a great, loving sigh, and he opened his arms to embrace them.

After they had all hugged each other, Mom said, "Children,

take Grandpa up to his room; he will want to bathe and change after his long journey. I'll go and make a nice cup of tea."

Sanjay began chattering as he clambered up the stairs, leading the way.

"Why aren't you wearing any shoes?" he asked.

"Because I took them off at the door, so as not to bring any dirt into the house. We always do that in India," answered Grandpa Chatterji.

"Did you come with lots of suitcases, Grandpa?" Sanjay went on, "and did you bring us lots of presents?"

"Ssh!" said Neetu, embarrassed. "That's rude, Sanjay."

"Just you wait and see," replied Grandpa, who didn't mind at all.

When they went into the guest room, they couldn't see any suitcases at all.

"Where is your luggage?" asked Neetu.

"Oh, I only ever travel with my bedroll," said Grandpa. "My needs are very simple," and he pointed to a roly-poly round khaki, canvas roll, all held together with leather straps, and covered in airline stickers and labels.

"Does that mean we don't have presents?" sighed Sanjay.

"Just you wait and see," replied Grandpa again.

"You've got the best room in the house," chattered Sanjay, bravely trying to ignore the mysterious roll which contained everything that Grandpa had brought.

"You've got the nicest sheets with duvet and curtains to match, you have the plumpest pillows and the softest bed. It's the best bed in the house for bouncing on," and Sanjay flung himself on to the bed, which Mom had made all smooth and neat, and he rumpled it all up.

"Sanjay!" cried Neetu with horror, dragging him off. "Look what you've done," and she tried to straighten it out.

"If you like this bed so much, you'd better sleep in it," said Grandpa Chatterji, "I prefer something harder."

"Where will you sleep then, Grandpa?" asked Neetu looking worried.

"I'll sleep on the floor as I always do," he replied. "I am like a snail, my dear," murmured Grandpa. "All I need, wherever I go, is my bedroll. It carries all my belongings, and when I unroll it, it becomes my bed."

The children looked in awe at the khaki, canvas roll. It suddenly seemed to be the most important thing in the world. "Can we unroll it, Grandpa?" whispered Sanjay.

Grandpa bent over the roll and undid the old leather straps, then he slowly unrolled it alongside the bed. At first it seemed that all it contained was one sheet and one blanket. Sanjay was sure there were no presents; but then Grandpa wriggled his hand into the large pocket at one end of the roll and pulled out a tooth mug and toothbrush all wrapped in a towel, a hair brush and comb and his shaving things. Sanjay stared expectantly. Were there any presents?

Then Grandpa went to a pocket at the other end and wriggled his hand inside. He pulled out a woolly jumper, a woolly hat, some socks, underwear, hankies, a shirt, tunic, and waistcoat, but still no presents.

At last, he folded back the sheet. Between the sheet and the blanket was a small, faded rug. He pulled back the rug to show lots of different packages.

"Presents!" breathed Sanjay, full of expectation.

"Why did you bring that old rug?" asked Neetu in a puzzled voice.

Grandpa Chatterji lifted it out as though it were the most precious thing in the world. "I never go anywhere without this," he murmured. "It is my meditation rug. I sit on it to do all my thinking and praying."

"Are those things presents?" asked Sanjay, pointing to the packages.

"Yes, yes, here you are," laughed Grandpa. He handed Sanjay two long thin packages.

"Thank you, thank you!" yelled Sanjay, ripping them open. "What are they?"

"One is a specially made, wooden wriggly snake, and the other is an Indian flute. Later I will teach you some tunes, but for now, you can just blow. It makes a lovely sound. Snakes love the sound of the flute. It makes them sway and puts them into a good mood."

Sanjay flung his arms round his old grandfather. "Thank you, thank you, Grandpa Chatterji!" and he rushed off to show his mom and dad.

Neetu waited patiently. Which package was for her? He bent over and handed her one of the larger ones. "What a beauty you are, my dearest, little granddaughter! This is for you!"

When Neetu opened up her package, she found a beautiful pink and green and gold sari. It was a special small-sized sari for little girls. In India they have to wait until they are nearly grown-up before they can wear a sari, but most little girls love to have a sari they can dress up in, and this is what her grandfather had brought for her.

It made Neetu feel very solemn and proud. "Oh thank you, Grandpa!" she declared in a grown-up voice, "I'll go and ask Mom to help me put it on."

Later, when Grandpa Chatterji had bathed and changed, Neetu, all dressed up in her sari, and Sanjay, with his snake and flute, went upstairs to find him. They knocked on his door.

"Come in!" he said in his soft, high voice.

They went in. Grandpa was sitting on the floor on his old rug. He was sitting very straight, his eyes staring in front and his arms stretched over his cross-legged knees.

"What are you doing, Grandpa?" asked Sanjay.

"I'm being a lotus flower floating quietly on a sea of milk."

"Why are you being a lotus flower?" asked Neetu. She was feeling beautiful and grown-up in her new sari.

Grandpa looked at her and smiled with admiration. "Come, children. Come and sit next to me. There's room on the rug."

Neetu and Sanjay sat cross-legged one on each side of their grandfather. They stretched out their arms over their knees and straightened their backs.

"We are being lotus flowers because we are trying to be as calm and peaceful and perfect as lotus flowers are," explained Grandpa Chatterji, "and if you close your eyes, you can imagine you are floating on a sea of milk before the creation of the world."

The children closed their eyes and floated away.

Then Grandpa suddenly woke up with a shout and cried, "I feel rested now! Come on! Where's that cup of tea your mother promised me? And while I'm drinking my tea, Sanjay can play the flute, and Neetu can dance! Will you?" he begged, his dark eyes glittering.

Neetu and Sanjay nodded with excitement. "Oh, Grandpa Chatterji! We're so glad you came."

Learning New Customs

Talk with your grandparents, parents, or guardians about a time when they had to learn new customs. Perhaps they came to Canada from another country and had to learn new ways. Or perhaps they have visited another country. Or perhaps they moved from a big city to a small town, or from one province to another. Did the differences between cultures cause problems? Did funny things happen? Collect their stories and share them with the class. Then discuss this question:

• Can kindness and friendliness (a large part of Grandpa Chatterji's character) overcome the differences between cultures?

IMAGINE!

After Grandpa Chatterji goes home, the children invite their Grandpa Leicester for dinner. Why? What happens?

If you enjoyed this story, you might want to read the whole novel! See More Good Reading on page 51 for details.

Understanding the Story

Visiting Grandpas

• Why do Neetu and Sanjay dislike their visits with Grandpa Leicester? Do you think their reasons are good?

• How does Grandpa Chatterji greet the children? What message does his greeting give them?

• What customs does Grandpa Chatterji demonstrate to the children. What reason does he give for each?

• Why do you think the children feel so comfortable with Grandpa Chatterji? Is it the presents he gives them, or something else?

Combining Sentences

When you're writing, short sentences are always good, but sometimes you want to combine sentences to show a connection between two ideas. For example, here are two sentences.

Sentence 1: Neetu and Sanjay don't like Grandpa Leicester's visits.
Sentence 2: Grandpa likes to eat vegetable curry and stuff like that.

If we combine the sentences using the linking word **because**, we can show the connection between them.

Combined sentence: Neetu and Sanjay don't like Grandpa Leicester's visits because Grandpa likes to eat vegetable curry and stuff like that.

Here are some linking words that are used in the story:
because   and   but   although   then
Try using them to combine the following sentences:

1. Mom's dad lives in India. Dad's dad lives in Leicester.

2. Neetu and Sanjay are a little afraid of Grandpa Leicester. They love and respect him as head of the family.

3. Grandpa Chatterji bent over the roll. He undid the old leather straps. He slowly unrolled it alongside the bed.

4. Grandpa Chatterji gave Neetu a beautiful sari. He gave Sanjay an Indian flute and a wooden snake.

Something To Think About!

Grandpa Chatterji shared his special way of meditating with his grandchildren. Thinking about being "a lotus flower floating quietly on a sea of milk" helped them to focus on being calm and peaceful.

Do you have a favourite image that would help you feel calm and peaceful? Try thinking about this image during a quiet time at home.

BEFORE READING

Dawa and Olana live in Mongolia. You can find Mongolia on a globe or world map, in northern China.

Read on to see if the boys achieve their dream—to have horses of their own.

Text and Photos by
Jan Reynolds

Dawa and

BOYS OF MONGOLIA

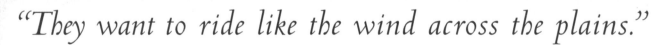

"They want to ride like the wind across the plains."

As the evening clouds sweep over the great plains of Mongolia, Dawa asks his father to tell him and his cousin Olana one more story. Dawa and Olana listen to Father's tales late into the night.

"Long ago your grandfather was given a young, high-spirited horse by his father. He cared for the horse and trained it to carry him like the wind across our wild plains. Mongolian horses are known far and wide as the swiftest and strongest of horses."

The candles burn down lower and lower as the night grows old. Dawa and Olana fall asleep dreaming about having horses of their own.

Olana

Working with Horses

The next morning, Father saddles up a horse for Dawa to use, and ties it outside the cluster of *gers,* round portable huts made of wood, felt, and canvas. Dawa's family and Olana's family always keep their gers next to Grandfather's. They all live together as one extended family, out on the land through the changing seasons, close to nature.

Father rides out to bring in the herd of horses the family owns. He wants to find two small horses for Dawa and Olana. The boys wait impatiently for the horses, while Olana's father tells them how important it is to have a well-trained horse. The family uses the horses to help round up the cows, goats, and sheep that provide them with meat, milk, leather, and wool.

While they talk of horses, Olana's mother is inside her ger, heating milk over the stove so she can make yogurt for the whole family, everyone living in the three gers.

Now it is time for Dawa to ride out to meet his father and help herd the horses up toward the gers. But first he needs some help untying the horse.

Father has had his eye on a colt, or a young male horse, for Dawa, and when he is close enough, he stretches forward with a long pole and rope to catch the horse.

Uncle also rides through the herd, searching for a colt for Olana. These two young horses will be trained to help the boys in their daily work. But for now Dawa and Olana must share a horse, and it is time for Olana to ride with his father to bring in the cows to be milked.

Dawa and Olana chase after the frisky calves and herd them to the pen. Dawa's mother lets the calves nurse before she and her sister begin the milking. They milk at dawn and dusk every day.

After the milking is done, Olana's mother walks the fields picking up dried dung from the horses and cows. Because Mongolians use what nature provides, nothing is considered waste. This dung will be burned in the stove for cooking and heating. Dawa helps by flattening fresh dung to dry it.

Olana knows that the sheep and goats will soon be herded to the gers, so he calls the dog over to help. The dog is useful in their work, but he is also for protection, to tell the family when anyone comes near the gers.

Dawa and Olana wait for the animals to come close so they can chase the goats into the milking pen. Then Dawa's father can catch a fat sheep for the family to have for dinner, and for several dinners to come.

Moving On

The time has come to move. The family packs up the gers into bundles and loads them onto camels or a horse-drawn cart.

They usually travel about thirty kilometres, moving every month or so to make sure they have fresh grass and water for their animals. In winter they gather together with other people and build a fence around their many gers to protect them from the blowing snow.

At the new home site, Grandfather fixes the roof, while Olana and his father knot the round wooden frame together. Everyone needs to help put the roof poles into place. Dawa's mother attaches the poles to the walls, which strengthens the ger against the wind.

Pressed animal hair, or felt, is wrapped around the frame and covered with canvas for warmth and protection from the rain. Dawa is glad to have *aaruul,* sweet cheese, drying on the roof again, so that he can sneak a treat when he is hungry.

In the new pasture the animals have plenty of fresh grass and water to keep them strong and healthy.

milk, to drink and gives thanks for the healthy horses that they all depend on. Like many Mongolians, he has learned that he is part of nature, connected by the spirit of life to the pastures, the sky, and the horses.

Dawa and Olana are very pleased and proud to have their own young horses to train, too. They want to ride like the wind across the plains just as their grandfather has, and as Mongolians have for as long as anyone can remember. ◈

Celebration!

Other Mongolians in the area come by to invite the family to a large celebration. These neighbours are very pleased with their herd of horses, especially the young ones. Dawa loves to see the young horses that have been brought together for branding—marking the horses with the same pattern as the rest of the herd. This family's mark is a triangle and will remain on the horse for life.

During the celebration the men ride some of the stallions, or male horses, that have not been trained. These horses buck and kick, trying to throw off their riders. The men compete to see how long each man can stay on the horse.

When the riding is over, everyone gathers in the host family's ger to sing and eat. The host, the owner of the branded horses, offers *koumiss,* fermented mare's

A Disappearing Way of Life

Mongolians live in the heart of the Asian continent, in a land of high mountains, lush grasslands, and harsh desert. They raise and train strong horses, which they ride to herd cows, sheep, and goats.

They move often, travelling from place to place in order to find fresh green pasture and plenty of water for their animals. They live in simple, round houses they can easily take apart and pack up into loads to be carried by their horses and camels.

But this ancient way of life is disappearing. Roads for trucks are being built across the country and permanent buildings constructed. Life is changing for Mongolians as their horses and portable homes are replaced. With my photographs, I have tried to capture the Mongolian way of life before it vanishes forever.

Jan Reynolds

FOLLOW UP

◆

Did the boys achieve their dream? Do you think you would enjoy this way of life? Which of their customs and activities would be fun? Which would be difficult for you?

➤ **Read more about Jan Reynolds on page 34.**

Meaning from Context

With a classmate, discuss the meaning of the underlined phrases. Use the clues in each sentence to help you.

1. Dawa's family and Olana's family live together as one <u>extended family</u>.

2. Because Mongolians use what nature provides, <u>nothing is considered waste</u>.

3. Like many Mongolians, he has learned that he is <u>part of nature</u>, connected by <u>the spirit of life</u> to the pastures, the sky, and the horses.

Understanding the Article

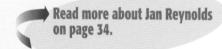

Cowhands of Asia

- Why are horses so important to the Mongolians? In what other regions or countries do you think horses are just as important? Examine the map at right.

- The Mongolians move every month or so, except in winter. How would you feel about moving so often?

- How are the jobs these boys do like the chores or jobs you do for your family?

- In the celebration only the men ride horses. Why do you think this is? Do you think this is fair? Explain your answer.

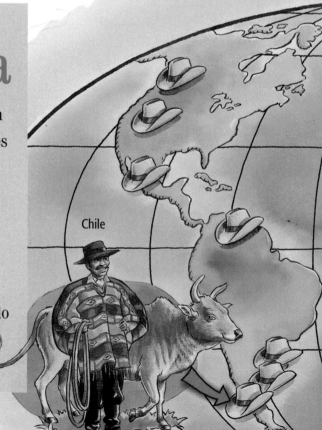

Chile

Reading for the Main Idea

Work with a partner to read the text on page 31, A Disappearing Way of Life. Discuss what the main idea is in each paragraph. For example, in the first paragraph the main idea is: Mongolians live and raise horses in the heart of Asia.

Write the main idea of the other paragraphs in your notebooks.

A Diary Entry

Imagine that you could spend a day in Mongolia with Dawa, Olana, and their families. What would you like to do there? Write a diary entry telling what you did in the morning, afternoon, and evening of your very special day.

TECH LINK
You could use a computer art program to add pictures or borders to your diary entry.

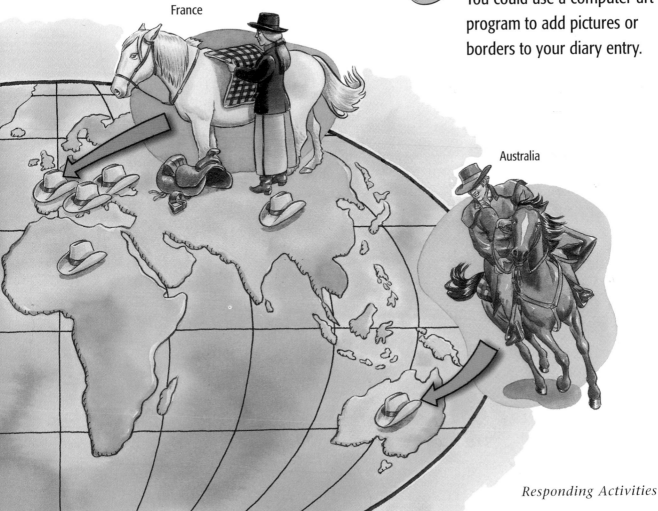

France

Australia

Dawa and Olana: Boys of Mongolia

Jan Reynolds

Interview by Susan Hughes
Photos by Jan Reynolds

Jan Reynolds does fascinating research! For each of her books she's travelled to a remote place to live with indigenous peoples–people who live close to nature and still follow a traditional way of life.

Susan: You must have lots of adventures on your travels.

Jan: I sure do! I've travelled to every continent—lived with the Laps in Lapland, the Aboriginals in Australia, and others. Wherever I go, I take notes and pictures.

Susan: How do you know what to photograph?

Jan: I try to photograph what goes on during the day. I play and work with the children and watch what they do.

Susan: When you went to Mongolia, how did you speak with the people?

Jan: I had a translator there. But I'll use sign language. Sometimes I don't understand everything. For example, when I take a trip with the people I'm visiting, I don't always know where we're going. That never stops me! I just go along for the ride.

Susan: What equipment do you take?

Jan: I pack a sleeping bag, first-aid kit, cameras, and lenses. I also take a tape recorder to record some of the sounds, and sometimes a video camera.

Susan: Did you ride horses with the boys, Dawa and Olana?

Jan: Absolutely! At first, they were worried that I was going to fall off. But I was fine. I'd been riding before.

Susan: Who travels with you?

An Inuit boy from Quamanituac (Baker Lake), Nunavut

Jan: Usually I travel alone. I'm away from my family for a few months, but I'm seldom lonely, and I meet wonderful people.

Susan: Could you tell me about someone special you met?

Jan: In Australia I met an Aboriginal woman who took me into a mangrove swamp, where there are crocodiles 10 m long and seven kinds of poisonous snakes! I explained to her that my next trip would be to the Amazon rainforest. When I got back home, there was a letter from her. The letter said, "Be careful on your trip!"

Susan: What important things have you learned while doing research?

Jan: Well, at first I thought I would find a lot of differences among peoples in faraway places. I began by going to the Himalayas and living with the Tibetans in their snowy mountains. Then I went to the Sahara Desert, expecting to meet completely different people. I discovered I had traded yaks for camels and snow for sand, but both peoples were living in much the same way. I learned that people may look different and have different customs—but basically we are all from the same human family.

A Samii girl,
Kautokeino, Norway

A Tiwi boy,
Bathurst Island,
Australia

Dawa and Olana with Jan Reynolds, Mongolia

BEFORE READING

These illustrations show the busy city of Cairo, Egypt. Examine them to see what Cairo looks like, and the kinds of jobs people do. Then read on to see what kind of job Ahmed does.

THE DAY OF
Ahmed's Secret

Story by Florence Parry Heide and Judith Heide Gilliland
Pictures by Ted Lewin

Today I have a secret, and all day long my secret will be like a friend to me.

Tonight I will tell it to my family, but now I have work to do in my city.

My donkey pulls the cart I ride on. I have many stops to make today. The streets are crowded. Everyone is going somewhere. Like me, everyone has something important to do.

And they are making such a noise of it!

All kinds of sounds, maybe every sound in the world, are tangled together: trucks and donkeys, cars and camels, carts and buses, dogs and bells, shouts and calls, and whistles and laughter all at once.

I have a sound, too, the sound my cart makes: *Karink rink rink, karink rink rink.* I know my sound helps to make the whole sound of the city, and it would not be the same without me.

Loudest of all to me today is the silent sound of my secret, which I have not yet spoken.

Over all the noise I hear my name, "Ahmed! Ahmed!" And my name becomes part of the city sound too.

It is Hassan calling to me. He leans over the counter of his cart, and the bright colours of the cart mingle with the other colours of the street, the way the noises all go together to make the sound of the city.

My special colours are part of the city, too. Woven into the harness of my donkey are my own good-luck ones, blue, green, and gold.

Hassan hands me a dish of beans and noodles and says, "And how goes the day of my friend the butagaz* boy?"

As I eat, Hassan and I laugh together at his jokes and stories. Always when I come home at sundown I tell his stories to my family, but tonight will be different. I will have my secret to tell them. I have been saving it until tonight.

Now someone else comes to Hassan's cart and I wave goodbye. I must hurry now if I am to get all my work finished today.

The first place I go is the home of the old woman. She has been waiting for me.

"Ahmed! Ahmed!" she calls. "Are you bringing me the fuel for my stove?"

---

* **Butagaz** is a word used to refer to the butane gas canisters used in gas stoves.

The old woman is leaning out of her window. I look up and smile. I am proud that I can carry these big heavy bottles all the way up the steps to the floor where she lives. I am proud that I can do this work to help my family.

I make more stops, and now I am hungry again. I look for the bright red and yellow cart where I can buy my lunch, and I find it in its usual place near the old building.

I buy my beans and rice, and sit in the shade of the old wall.

My father has told me the wall is a thousand years old, and even our great-great-grandfathers were not yet born when it was built. There are many old buildings, many old walls like the one I lean against, in this city.

I close my eyes and have my quiet time, the time my father says I must have each day. "If there are no quiet spaces in your head, it fills with noise," he has told me.

He has shown me how to find my way in the city, and he has taken me to each place where I now have to bring the heavy bottles.

In those days before I was strong enough to do this work alone, I would sit in the cart and watch my father lift and carry the bottles. One day I told him that now I could do it by myself. He watched me try to take a heavy bottle from the cart. I could not do it, and I was ashamed.

"Hurry to grow strong, Ahmed," my father said on that day. For the first time I saw that his face had a tired look, like the faces of the old men in the city.

"Hurry to grow strong," he said again. "But do not hurry to grow old."

Now as I lean against the old building, I think of the sea of sand that lies along our city. I have seen it, stretching as far as the wind.

My father says the wind carries sand all through the city to remind us that the desert is there, is there beside us, and is a part of us.

He tells me that the great desert presses against our city on one side, and the great river pushes against it on the other.

"We live between them," my father has said. "Between our two friends, the river and the desert."

All over the world, people know of our city, he tells me, and they speak its name: Cairo. And they say the name of our great river, the Nile.

"And the desert, what is that called?" I ask.

My father shrugs and smiles. "The hot winds call our desert home."

He himself has never crossed the desert. But in the city are the caravans of camels and their riders who have crossed it many times, the way the boats cross and recross the river.

The Day of Ahmed's Secret **39**

I lean against the wall and I think of these things and of my secret, but I must finish my work before I go home.

First I try to knock the sand from my sandals. The sand is a part of each day, like the noise, like the colours of the city, like the things my father has said.

On the way to my next stop I see the boy who carries bread.

From a window a girl lowers a basket to him on a rope, and he puts some bread in the basket. Like me, he has many stops to make each day, but he is not strong enough to do what I do. No one lowers a rope to me for my heavy loads! No rope could carry what I carry.

I hear the rosewater* man before I see him. He clicks two cups together as he walks along the street so people will hear him and come to him for a drink.

---

* **Rosewater** is water in which rose petals have been soaked or steeped. It tastes faintly of roses, and is a very popular drink.

I give him my smile. He does not give me his, but our eyes meet and we know we are connected to the same day and to the city.

I do not buy his rosewater, but seeing him has reminded me how hot and thirsty I am. I take a drink from the bottle of water I always carry in my cart.

There are more stops to make, and more times up and up narrow steps with my heavy load, and then I am back in my cart.

Karink rink rink, karink rink rink.

It is a long day. I think the moment will never come when I may share my secret, but of course I know that each day ends and that every moment has its time to be.

Finally I am home. It is sundown, it is the time of day when you cannot tell a white thread from a black one. My mother has already lighted the lanterns. Everyone is waiting for me.

Instead of telling them about my day, I say, "Look, I have something to show you."

It is time to tell my secret. I take a deep breath.

"Look," I say. "Look, I can write my name."

I write my name over and over as they watch, and I think of my name now lasting longer than the sound of it, maybe even lasting, like the old buildings in the city, a thousand years. ◈

What is Ahmed's job? How does he feel about the work he does?

A Character Portrait

Ahmed is a character in a story, but the author really brings him to life. What qualities does he have that would make him a good friend? Your goal is to write a paragraph describing Ahmed. Here is a process you could follow:

Prepare

1. List Ahmed's qualities.

2. After each quality you listed, write at least one example from the story.

Write

3. Write a **topic sentence** to begin your paragraph. This sentence tells the reader what you are going to write about. **Indent** your topic sentence.

4. Turn your lists of qualities and examples into sentences. Arrange them in order (for example, from least important to most important).

5. Write a **concluding sentence** that sums up your feelings about Ahmed.

Revise and proofread

6. Read your paragraph quietly to yourself. Change anything that sounds funny or confusing. Check your spelling. That's it! You've written a good paragraph.

> **IMAGINE!**
> How do you think Ahmed learned his "secret"? Share your idea with others. How many different ideas do you have?

Understanding the Selection

What's the Secret?

- Who are Ahmed's friends in the city? What does he do with each one?

- Ahmed's father gives him some advice: "Hurry to grow strong...but do not hurry to grow old." What do you think he means?

- What is Ahmed's special secret? Why is he so excited about it?

- How did you feel when you first learned to write your name?

The 28 Characters in the Arabic Alphabet

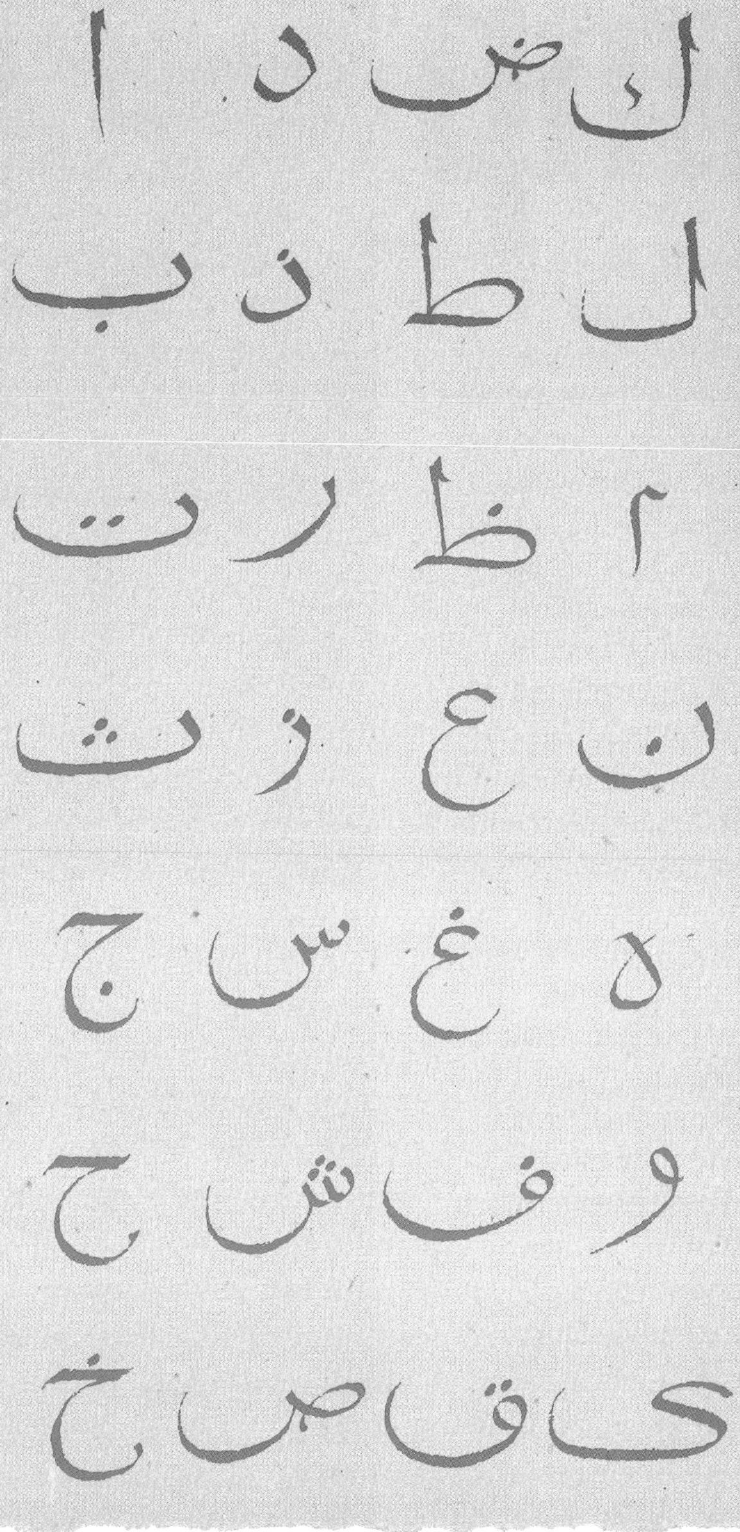

ا د ض ل

ل ن ط ل

ت ر ظ ٢

ث د ع ن

ج س غ ه

ح ش ف و

خ ص ق ى

Did You Know ?

Ahmed uses the Arabic alphabet to write his name. This alphabet was created around A.D. 512, and is one of the most widely used alphabets in the world. It has 28 letters, and is read from right to left. Arabic words used in English include *algebra*, *alfalfa*, and *albatross*.

SENSORY DETAILS

As Ahmed tells this story he includes many details that appeal to the reader's five senses. Which senses do you think are the most important to Ahmed? Why?

In your notebook fill in a chart like the one below, with examples from the story. Compare your finished chart with a classmate's.

Sight	Sound	Taste	Touch	Smell
camels carts			wind	

TIP > Your own writing can improve when you use lots of sensory details!

BEFORE READING

Read the title and look at the photos in this article. Write down two or three questions that come to your mind. Then read the text to look for the answers.

Poems and Photos by
CHILDREN FROM GUATEMALA

Edited by
KRISTINE L. FRANKLIN and NANCY McGIRR

Out OF THE Dump

About 1500 people, mostly children, live in the garbage dump in Guatemala City. They work hard collecting plastic, glass, and tin for recycling. Nancy McGirr wanted to help these children, so she started a project in which the kids photograph their world. She brought cameras to the dump and let any child who wanted to take pictures. Soon twenty-three children had joined the project. Kristine Franklin also joined to help the children with their writing.

Using their photos, the children make notecards, prints, and books, which they sell to make money. Because they can help their families this way, their parents can afford to let them go to school. Already they have a better life. In the future, some of the children hope to work as photographers and writers.

> **For these children, photography has become a door to an exciting new world alive with possibilities. It is a door they have opened.**
>
> *Nancy McGirr*

Donna in Our Alley
by Marta Lopez

Our Alley

Poem by Marta Lopez

Three little houses
  guard our alley.
Three little houses
    full of children:
    five in my house,
      three behind,
      four across the alley.
We share the alley:
    it's where we play,
      where we walk,
      where we listen
      to people who fight.
We share the alley,
    but the clothesline?
      No!
My sister climbs a pole
    to hang the wet clothes.
      Later
    she stands guard
      so no one steals
      the clothes.
We share the alley,
    but the clothesline
      is ours.

The Spider

Poem by Junior Ramos

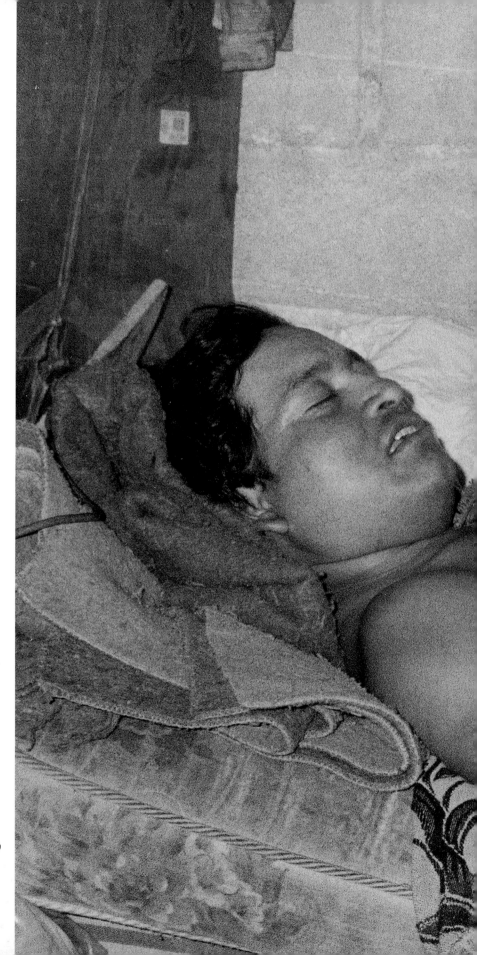

The biggest spider
in the world.
I found it
in the house under my bed,
lurking in the shadows.

The biggest spider
in the world.
I found it,
a black one with spots,
hunting for food.

The biggest spider
in the world.
I caught it
and put it on my stepdad
sleeping on the bed.

The biggest spider
in the world.
I scared my mom.
My stepdad didn't wake up
even when she screamed.

The biggest spider
in the world.
My brother tore off
all of its legs and now
my rubber joke is dead.

My stepfather taking a nap
by Junior Ramos

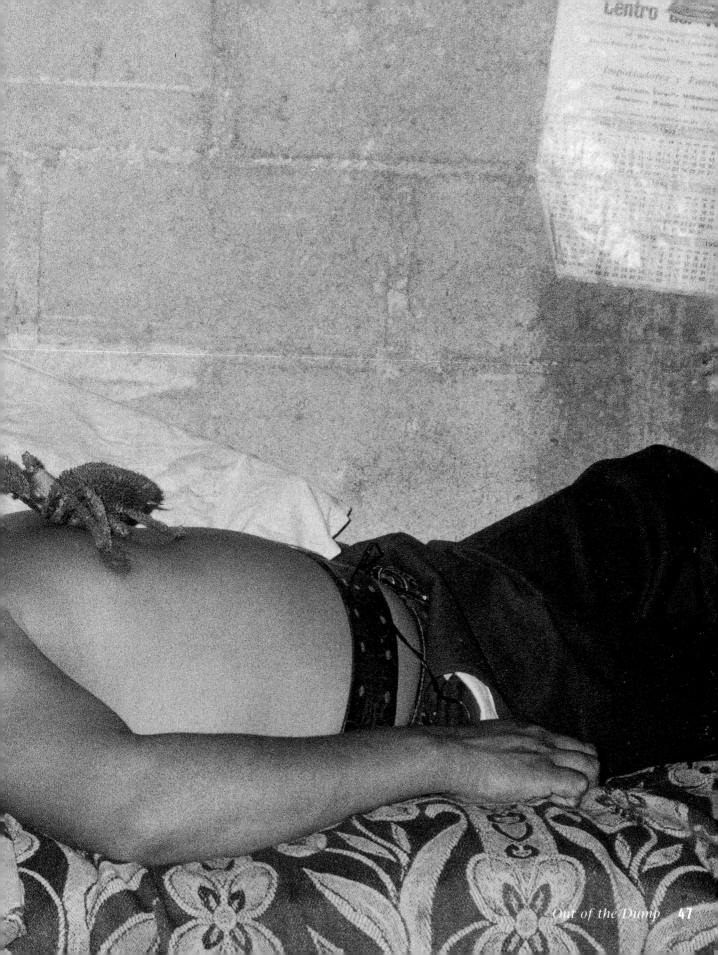

Reading Lesson

Poem by Gladiz Jimenez

Our teacher teaches us the vowels.
If we don't learn them
she repeats
A E I O U
until we have them memorized
frontwards and backwards.
The lesson called "mama"
goes like this:
ma me mi mo mu.
"Repeat it," says the teacher;
and we do, and then
we learn to write Mama,
the most important word.
I want to read it all,
stories, books,
signs in the street,
the menu in a restaurant.
But before I read
I must review
ma me mi mo mu.
My parents can't read.
They can only write
their names.
Maybe I
will be their teacher.
Ma me mi mo mu.

My mother
by Gladiz Jimenez

Marta Lopez, ten, has helped with children's photo workshops in Great Britain and wants to be a teacher.

Junior Ramos, fourteen, wants to continue with his photography and hopes to work as a photojournalist.

Gladiz Jimenez, thirteen, is the first of the group to start junior high school. She is also apprenticing* as a photographer with an international news agency.

Rosario Lopez, twelve, is apprenticing with an international news agency. She and her sister Marta are helping to support their family since their father died.

* **Apprentice:** to work with skilled people to learn a trade or craft

FOLLOW UP

Did you find answers to the questions you wrote down?

What is the most important thing you learned from reading the article and viewing the photos?

Viewing Photos

Here's what Junior Ramos has to say about taking pictures.

In the photography class they taught me to take pictures. First I learned to put the film in the camera. Then I learned that the most important things to remember are the angle and the lighting. After that, I learned to take photographs.

I like taking pictures of parties best, because at a party everyone is dancing. Watching people dance makes me want to dance too. The music is always happy, with a rock beat. When I take a picture of the sound equipment, I am taking a picture of the music itself. That way I can remember the party forever. I want to take pictures for the rest of my life.

Work with a small group. Look closely at the photos in the article, then discuss two or three of the ideas below. Choose one person in the group to share your responses with the class.

- Choose one photo and imagine what a person is thinking about.
- Find a photo that shows a strong contrast between light areas and dark areas. Where is the light coming from?
- Imagine you have stepped into one of the photos. What sounds do you hear? What can you touch? What can you taste or smell?
- Pick one photo and discuss why the photographer took it from the angle he or she used (high-angle, low-angle, wide-angle, or close-up). What effect does this angle have on the viewer?

Dancing
by Rosario Lopez

Sharing the Alley

- What would you say to these children if you could meet them?

- What did you learn from the children's writing and photos about the way they live?

- Do you think the photography project for the children was a good idea? Why?

- Why is *Out of the Dump* a good title for the article?

Media Link

Create a photo essay

A photo essay uses mainly photographs to present information about a subject. You can create a photo essay by taking your own photos, or by cutting out photos from newspapers and magazines. Place the photos in order so that your photo essay has a beginning, a middle and an end. Paste them into a scrapbook or onto Bristol board. If you wish, add words (captions) below the photos. Here are some possible topics for your photo essay:

my family

school days

poverty

celebrations

disasters

MORE GOOD READING

Children Just Like Me
by Barnabas and Anabel Kindersley
Wonderful photos and text introduce you to a whole wide world of kids: including Esta, from Tanzania; Levi, from northern Canada; and Rachel, from France. (a photo-information book)

River My Friend
by William Bell
Gang-gang, the son of a skillful fisher in China, dreams of fishing for silver coins to help his family escape poverty. (a picture book)

The Distant Talking Drum
by Isaac Olaleye
These poems are about life in a Nigerian village—children's games, tropical storms, and farmers' markets. Colourful paintings bring the words to life! (poetry collection)

Tal Niv's Kibbutz
by Allegra Taylor
Ten-year-old Tal Niv lives with his family on a Kibbutz in Israel—a community where 300 people live and work together. (a photo-information book)

Grandpa Chatterji
by Jamila Gavin
Neetu and Sanjay's relationship with their Grandpa Chatterji continues in this novel. Check it out for more adventures and heartwarming episodes! (novel)

ENJOY THE EARTH

Yoruba, Africa

Enjoy the earth gently
Enjoy the earth gently
For if the earth is spoiled
It cannot be repaired
Enjoy the earth gently

THIS LAND

Akawaio, South America

This land is where we belong
This land is where we are at home, we know its ways
This land is needed for those who come after
We know where to find all this land provides for us
This land keeps us together within its mountains

BEFORE READING

Would you expect to find a scientist up in a tree fort? Read on to find out why bug scientists have a research station at the top of a tree, and what they do there.

MAGAZINE ARTICLE BY
Faron Nicholas
AND
Douglas Cowell

Going Buggy in the Trees

There are some very lucky scientists in British Columbia. They actually get paid to climb trees.

My name is Faron Nicholas. I'm in grade seven in Victoria, British Columbia, and I love climbing trees, too. Last November I was invited to climb to the tops of some very huge trees to see just what those scientists do up there.

We went to a place called Rocky Point near where I live. That's a rocky, hilly piece of land on the southern tip of Vancouver Island. The scientists have a canopy research station there in the middle of a very rare forest of big, old Douglas fir trees. The canopy is the top part of a forest—the part with all the leaves or needles. The scientists climb Douglas firs that are 40 to 50 m tall to find out exactly what kinds of animals live up there.

When I got to the station, Nancy Prockiw, a scientist, and Kevin Jordan, a professional tree climber, told me about Canada's Biodiversity Accord. It is a promise that Canada made to the world a few years ago that not a single species in this country would ever get wiped out, or extirpated*. Well, before Canada can keep that promise we need to know exactly what species live here. Nancy and Kevin and other scientists across the country are trying to discover every animal and plant species we have.

Ant

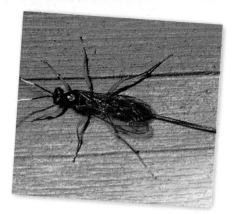

Not yet identified

Kevin is the one who built the station. At the bottom of the tree I was going to climb, he showed me both ends of a long white rope. It seemed to hang down from somewhere high above. Then he helped me put on a climbing harness. It was a series of strong nylon bands that wrapped around my legs, waist, and shoulders. Kevin insisted there was no way I could fall out of it.

Kevin went up the rope first and sent the loose end back down. Then it was my turn. I clipped my harness onto the rope with a metal link called a carabiner (KARE-ah-been-er). I wasn't scared when I looked way, way up that tree, but it's a seriously high tree—way higher than any roller coaster I've ever been on.

Aphids

---

*extirpated** means to be completely destroyed.

There was nothing for me to hold on to, I was just hanging there in the air. All alone, I rose higher and higher, spinning around slowly, dangling like a spider. It was exciting.

Once I had floated past some branches I could see Kevin waiting for me further up on a tiny platform strapped to the tree (*see photo on page 54*). He helped me get onto the platform and clipped me onto a safety line. Everywhere I went there were safety lines. As long as I hooked myself onto one properly, the way Kevin showed me, I would always be safe.

Above us on the tree were two more platforms. We could climb up to them on ladders that were strapped to the tree trunk.

Soon Nancy was up and began doing her research. She removed a bottle from a contraption that looked like a pup tent (*below*) but was made of fine netting. It's called a Malaise trap and it catches flying insects in a jar of alcohol so the scientists can study them back in the laboratory.

Nancy (*above*) and the other bug scientists she works with (called **entomologists**) are trying to discover all the kinds of arthropods that live in the treetops. Arthropods, like crabs, spiders, and millipedes, are animals with jointed legs and hard outer shells. The largest group of arthropods is insects. Plants, animals, and people live together in groups called ecosystems. Nancy wants to learn how the arthropods found here fit into the canopy ecosystem.

So far Nancy and the other scientists have caught about one and a half million bugs. Oops! I mean arthropods. They've already listed about 1300 different species, and 100 of them have never been seen before. Scientists around the world were surprised at that.

While Kevin and Nancy went about their work, I climbed around the station looking at things. I saw that the platforms were tied in place with big straps. I really liked that because it meant that they didn't hammer a single nail into the tree. They didn't hurt the tree at all.

They told me that bugs aren't the only things that live up here. Kevin has climbed more than 5000 big trees and has even slept overnight on the platforms. He's seen mice, squirrels, hummingbirds, and even slugs high in the canopy.

Finally, it was time to leave. I clipped onto the rope and slid down, down, into the darkness below. It felt good to stand on the ground again.

I learned some interesting things about the natural world and discovered a little bit about the work these scientists do. I think they have a great job. I mean, these guys work in the coolest tree fort a kid could hope for. ◆

Spider (unidentified)

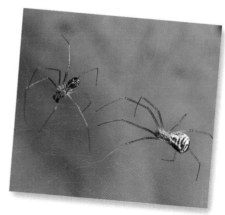

Combfooted spider

FOLLOW UP

Why do you think it's important for scientists to climb trees? What do they do at the top of the tree that they couldn't do anywhere else?

Understanding the Article

A Forest Ecosystem

- What kind of scientist is Nancy? What equipment does she use to help her do her research?

- Why are Nancy Prockiw and other scientists trying to discover every animal and plant species in Canada? Do you think they'll be successful? Explain your answer.

- What do you think was the most important thing Faron learned from his experience?

- Would you like to have an adventure like Faron's? Why or why not?

- Would you like to be a "bug" scientist? What would you like most about this job? What would you like least?

IMAGINE!

You're in charge of naming new bugs. What would you call the bug at the top of page 55?

Buggy Words

Do you know what these words mean?

arthropod   **laboratory**   **entomologist**
ecosystem   **species**   **extirpated**

To discover their meaning read the article again, looking for clues. Then check a dictionary and find out how to pronounce the words, too!

Your Local Ecosystem

Going Buggy in the Trees explains that plants, animals, and people live together in groups called **ecosystems**. Think about where you live. Do you live near the ocean? in a city? on the Prairies? in the Far North? With four or five classmates, discuss ecosystems and decide which ecosystem you are part of. Make a list of the plants and animals that also live in your ecosystem. Then discuss how the people, plants, and animals are connected to each other. Present your ideas to the class.

TIP Assign different roles to each person in the group. For example: discussion leader, note-taker, researcher, presenter.

"Guess the Bug" Game

1. Look closely at the photos of the insects (arthropods) that live in the forest canopy. Observe their size, shape, colours, and any other interesting features.

2. Choose the insect you think is most interesting and write a description of it. List descriptive details in point form first. Then write the information as a paragraph. DON'T include the name of your insect.

3. In groups of four, take turns reading your descriptions. If you have written an accurate description, your classmates should be able to guess the name of your bug!

4. Share your description and this article with your family. Challenge them to "Guess the Bug"!

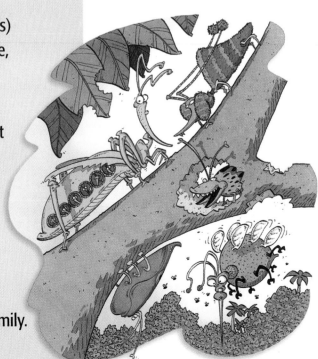

Something To Think About

Scientists want to learn everything they can about the plant and animal species in the forest canopy. Do you think this knowledge will lead to the protection of these species? Why or why not?

 TECH LINK
Post your thoughts on your school's home page. Start a dialogue with other web users about this subject.

Poem for the Ancient Trees

I
am young and
I want to live
to be old
and I don't want to
outlive these trees — this forest.
When my last song is gone
I want these same trees
to be singing on — newer green songs
for generations to come
so let me be old — let me grow
to be ancient
to come as an elder
before these same temple-green sentinels
with my aged limbs
and still know a wonder
that will outlast me.
O I want
long love
long life.
Give me
150 years
of luck.
But don't
let me
outlive
these trees.

Poem by
**Robert
Priest**

Picture by
**Bernadette
Lau**

A Shape Poem

Poem for the Ancient Trees is a shape poem —a poem that is shaped like its subject, a tree. In shape poems, the way the words appear on the page is as important as the words and their meaning.

Think about a tree you know and love. Make a list of its features—size, shape, colour. Make another list of the creatures that live in it, climb it, or fly to it. Then use this information to write your own shape poem.

TIP > To get the shape you want, experiment with the length of your lines, and the size of your words. Complete several different drafts to see what works best.

Understanding the Poem

Tree Appreciation

- Why do you think Robert Priest chose this shape for his poem?

- Many people want to live forever, but Priest doesn't want to outlive the ancient trees. Why not?

- Priest calls the ancient trees "temple-green sentinels." What do you think he means? What do you think the colour "temple-green" looks like?

RESEARCH

Old Growth Forests

Ancient trees form a special ecosystem called "old-growth forests." These old forests have never been logged, so they contain a variety of trees, from young to old. Fallen trees decay on the forest floor, providing homes for all sorts of animals and plants.

Research to find out more about old-growth forests. You could use your library, encyclopedias, the Internet, or environmental organizations. Present your information using pictures and captions.

 TECH LINK Using multimedia tools can really bring your research to life!

ApeS ON the

Profile and Experiment by **Jay Ingram**   Pictures by **Dan Hobbs**

As far back as Biruté Galdikas can remember, she always loved orangutans. When she was growing up, she read about these apes in books and watched them at the local zoo. She thinks one of the reasons they appealed to her was their calmness, their slow and unhurried life.

Today Biruté spends part of her time teaching in British Columbia, but her heart is in Indonesia.

Go

Dr. Biruté Galdikas,
anthropologist

She runs Camp Leakey in the Indonesian part of the island of Borneo. There she and her researchers follow orangutans day in and day out and study their habits to learn more about these mysterious animals. And she's convinced they do indeed live a blissfully slow and easy life in the treetops.

It's not easy tracking orangutans and recording the details of their lifestyle, even though Biruté has been doing this work for twenty years. You have to follow them as they move. If they're in the trees, they're hard to miss, but once they get on the ground, Biruté says, "they can just vanish!" And chasing orangutans in the Borneo jungle means working in incredible heat and humidity, and having your blood sucked by disease-carrying insects, among other things.

You can do exactly the same sort of research Biruté does, without ever leaving your neighbourhood. Track a human the way she tracks an orangutan, and write up your own research report, called a **time budget**.

Making a Time Budget

1 Choose a subject: your sister, brother, parent, or another person who lives with you. Don't choose someone outside your family since you won't be around them enough to study them.

2 List the activities you expect your subject to do, such as eating, playing, watching television, working, reading, talking, and sleeping (both napping and at night).

3 Now, watch your subject. Biruté and her team usually follow the same orangutan for ten days, watching it from when it gets out of the nest in the morning to the time it beds down in a new nest at night. If it's not practical for you to follow your subject that closely, try to do just a few hours at a time. And for best results, don't let your subject see you watching.

4 As you watch, write down the amount of time your subject spends on each activity. You can add up the minutes later and show your results on a graph.

The scientists watching orangutans at Camp Leakey record their research on a graph something like the one you see here.

See how your human subject's daily activities compare with a typical orangutan's. This graph shows roughly how a young orangutan, about the age of an eight- to twelve-year-old human, spends its day.

After 12 hours of sleep, it's up at dawn, 6:00 a.m. or so. Until sundown, 12 hours later, there will be about 21/2 hours of moving through the jungle (mostly looking for food), another 21/2 hours of resting with some play, and about 7 hours of snacking!

You probably won't find any of your subjects spending 7 hours eating. But you might be surprised to find out just how humans do spend their time. ◆

Understanding the Selection

Going Ape

- Why do you think Biruté Galdikas has devoted 20 years to studying orangutans in the wild?

- Biruté Galdikas is very concerned about preserving the habitat of the orangutans. What problems do you think the animals might be facing?

- What is the advantage of recording research on a graph?

- What did you find was the most difficult part of completing your time budget?

Wildlife TV Show

Imagine you're a filmmaker who's been sent to the jungle to spend time with Biruté Galdikas and the orangutans. Create an outline for the TV show you would produce.

Personal Response

Have you decided which family member you plan to observe? Make predictions about how the activities of the person you watch will compare with the activities of the orangutans.

Make a Graph

Make a **Time Budget** bar graph based on your typical school day.

What conclusions can you draw from the information on your graph? Compare your graph with those of other students'.

 TECH LINK
Use a computer spreadsheet to help you graph your data.

Think of the Ocean...

Poem by Siobhan Swayne   Picture by Heather Holbrooke

think of the ocean
      as a cat
with her grey fur
         pushed
     high upon her back
      white boots
      kneading the shore
          on stormy days.
but
  with the sun
    shining
in a silk blue sky
    she purrs
 softly and her fur is
   licked smooth and green
like the sand stone
      she sleeps upon.

Personal Response

Poets love to surprise readers with their comparisons. Were you surprised that Siobhan Swayne compared the huge, limitless ocean to a cat? How does her ocean/cat change moods between verse one and verse two?

POET'S CRAFT

Similes

As Strong As an Ox

The comparison in this poem is called a simile. Similes compare different things using the words "like," "than," or "as." For example, "think of the ocean/as a cat." Can you find another simile in the poem?

Why do poets use similes? They may want you to see something in a new way. Or they may want to show how two very different things can be similar in some ways.

In your notebook, develop some similes of your own:

Think of the forest as a _____ .
My city is like a _____ .
My best friend is as _____ **as a** _____ .

Continue this list with more similes for common things.

TIP > Remember to use similes next time you write a poem, a story, or anything at all!

Information Guide by
Pamela Hickman

Pictures by
Twila Robar-DeCoste

Atlantic Seashore

An outing to the seashore is a great way to have fun and meet some of nature's most fascinating creatures. Whether you dig in the mud, poke into rock pools, paddle in the shallows, or just lie on the beach, many new adventures await you at the shore.

Tide Talk

There are two tides per day on the Atlantic shore. It is a bit longer than six hours between high tide and low tide. Certain shorelines, particularly along the Bay of Fundy and Minas Basin, have extremely high tides that come in very quickly. The best time to explore the shorelines below the cliffs in these areas is after high tide, when the tide is going out.

When you go down to the shore, look for the high tide mark along the sand or rocks. You can usually see a line of seaweed, driftwood, and other things that have been left high and dry by the water. On large rocks, you may be able to see a difference in the kinds of plants and animals that are attached above and below the high tide mark.

Check the local tourist bureau or newspaper for the current tide times in your area. Tide times change 50 minutes from one day to the next. For example, if high tide comes at 6:00 a.m. and 6:25 p.m. on one day, it will come again at approximately 6:50 a.m. and 7:15 p.m. the next day.

Beachcombing

When you're looking for shells on the beach, you will likely come across a number of other plant and animal remains that have been washed up by the wind and the waves. Look for these common beach "finds" and others.

SAND DOLLARS

Look for dried, bleached sand dollars. The round, hard shells of these animals are often used as decorations. Notice the five "petals" radiating from a central hole on the top. Turn the shell over to find the mouth hole in the centre.

CRAB SHELLS

Bits and pieces of crab shells often turn up in the sand. As crabs grow, they shed their old shell and grow a new one. The old shells are discarded and wash up on beaches.

EYED FINGER–SPONGES

You may come across a piece of bleached spongy material with many finger-like branches and eye-like markings. Sponges look a bit like plants but they are really animals. If you have a hand lens, look closely at the pores covering the sponge. The sponge filters food out of the water that flows through the pores.

SEAWEED

Most seaweed grows attached to rocks underwater, but it often breaks off and is washed up on beaches. Try popping the balloon-like air bladders of bladder wrack (rockweed) and knotted wrack, or wrap yourself in long ribbons of kelp.

SKATE EGG CASES

If you find a small black, leathery "pouch" with long, curled spines, you've found the egg case of a skate. Also known as a mermaid's purse, the pouch contained the eggs and developing young of a skate, a fish with a long tail and wing-like fins that lives close to the ocean floor.

JELLYFISH

If you happen to find a jellyfish washed up on the beach, do not touch it because its tentacles can still sting several hours after the animal has died. Jellyfish get their name from the strong, jelly-like substance that forms their body.

Sand Tracks and Trails

When the tide is out, take a walk across the wet sand. What kinds of markings do you see in the sand? Some are left by the receding water, while others are signs of life at the shore. On your next visit to the beach, see how many of these signs you can find.

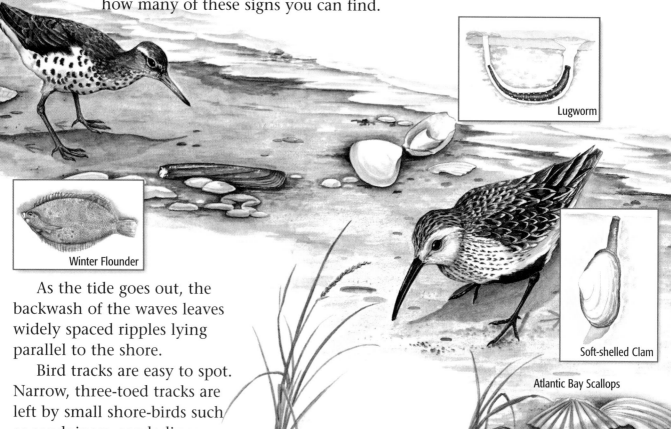

Lugworm

Winter Flounder

Soft-shelled Clam

Atlantic Bay Scallops

As the tide goes out, the backwash of the waves leaves widely spaced ripples lying parallel to the shore.

Bird tracks are easy to spot. Narrow, three-toed tracks are left by small shore-birds such as sandpipers, sanderlings, and plovers. If you see large, triangular webbed feet, they are probably seagulls' imprints. Deep, narrow holes near shorebird tracks are made when the birds poke their beaks into the mud while feeding. Shorebirds find their food by feeling and smelling it.

Small, shallow depressions in the sand are signs of flounder. They come in with the tide and take "bites" out of the sand in their search for food in the mud.

Lugworms live in the sand in the intertidal zone—the area between the high and low tide marks. With some

practice you can find their tiny U-shaped burrows. The front opening is funnel-shaped and the narrower back opening is marked by tiny piles of castings, similar to the castings of earthworms.

If you notice water squirting out of groups of holes in the sand or mud as you approach, you have probably found a colony of soft-shelled clams. They are often found near a freshwater inlet. Razor clams also squirt water and then quickly burrow deeper into the sand.

At low tide look for the outlines of bar clams buried just below the surface.

S.O.S. Save our Shorelines

You have discovered some of the amazing variety of plants and animals that call the seashore home. These plants and animals depend on each other for survival, but none can survive without their habitat.

Whether it's a rocky shore, sandy beach, mudflat, or saltmarsh, the destruction of a habitat leads to the loss of the species that live there.

Some of the major threats to shoreline species include pollution from oil spills, toxic chemicals, garbage, and motor vehicles. Several endangered species, including the piping plover, leatherback turtle, and northern right whale depend on healthy shorelines and water for their survival. You can help protect the shoreline and its wildlife by following these conservation tips.

Leatherback Turtle

Conservation Tips

1. Always take your garbage away with you. Pack an extra plastic bag so you can pick up garbage left by others and make the shoreline a better place for everyone.

2. Handle living creatures carefully. When you are finished looking at them, always return them to where you found them.

3. If you find a nest, watch it from a safe distance and make sure that the adult birds or animals are not frightened away. Do not touch the nest, eggs, or young.

4. Enjoy the wildflowers where they grow, instead of picking them.

5. Do not climb on sand dunes. They are very sensitive to disturbance and can be easily damaged by trampling.

6. It is illegal to dig and remove fossils from the shoreline cliffs and reefs.

Piping Plover

Did this selection include any of the things you've seen or found on the seashore? What new information did you learn?

Discovering Our Parks

There are several national parks located along the Atlantic shore. Working with two or three classmates, choose one of the parks listed at right and research what sea creatures can be found there, and what the seashore is like. Create a visual display inviting visitors to discover the park.

Newfoundland and Labrador
- Gros Morne National Park

New Brunswick
- Fundy National Park
- Kouchibouguac National Park

Nova Scotia
- Cape Breton Highlands National Park

Prince Edward Island
- Prince Edward Island National Park

Québec
- Parc National Forrillon

 TECH LINK
Visit the parks on-line, by going to the Parks Canada Web site.

Understanding the Guide

Ecosystem on the Beach

- Which of these things is a fish?

jellyfish   crab   skate   seaweed   sponge   sand dollar

- What creature makes each of these kinds of tracks and trails?

U-shaped burrows   three-toed tracks   shallow depressions

- Why should you visit shorelines below the cliffs after high tide?

- List three kinds of habitats that exist on the seashore. Why is it important to preserve these habitats?

YOUR TURN TO WRITE

A Letter to the Editor

Suppose you were visiting the seashore and you saw that lots of people had left their litter behind. You can always write to the editor of the local newspaper to complain. Here's an example of a letter to the editor:

> Dear Editor,
>
> On my last visit to the beach, I was shocked to see people walking away from their empty pop bottles and fast-food packages.
>
> Don't they realize that leaving a mess encourages other people to do the same? Even worse, litter spoils the beach habitat for nesting birds. So please, beach-goers, next time take along a bag and remove your garbage!
>
> Craig Mayerovich, Sydney, Nova Scotia

You can also write letters to the editor to praise someone, inform people, disagree with another letter writer, or tell an interesting story. To write your own letter follow these steps:

1. Bring copies of local newspapers to class and read the letters to the editor.

2. Think of a topic you would like to write about. List your main points.

3. Write a first draft, then exchange with a partner. Remember, you want to convince people that you have a good point to make!

4. When your letter is polished, you can send it to the newspaper. Maybe it will be published!

MEET THE AUTHOR

Pamela Hickman

Interview by Susan Berg

Pamela Hickman, author of *At the Seashore,* has a goal: to get kids hooked on nature through her books. "The more you learn about nature the more fascinating it becomes, and the more new things you want to learn," she claims.

Pamela's interest in nature began when she was a child in Ontario, playing in her own backyard. She also learned a lot from camping trips with her parents, her sister and two brothers.

"I got the chance to see Canada from coast to coast and up into the Arctic," says Pamela. "When I was only four or five years old, I remember watching a large black bear wander through our camp in a national park in British Columbia!"

Now Pamela lives on Minas Basin, near the Bay of Fundy in Nova Scotia. She still goes camping, along with her husband and her three daughters, aged seven to eleven. "We love to camp in Kejimcujik National Park. You can go canoeing, and there are lots of lakes warm enough to swim in. Around here, you can't swim in the Atlantic Ocean. It's too cold!"

Pamela finds material for her books in her nearby surroundings. "I go beachcombing all year-round," she boasts. "I can spend all day at the seashore and not see another person. But I see lots of different birds, seals, and even deer."

The shore is a really special habitat. It's also a great place for finding fossils, agates (a type of crystal stone with many different-coloured stripes), and amethysts (a purple- or violet-coloured crystal stone).

Pamela has written over twenty books for kids. "My own kids think it's neat that I'm a writer," says Pamela. "They get excited whenever another book is published. They also give me ideas for new books. When I visit classrooms, I take my

> About nature, Pamela Hickman says:
>
> **"You can't love and want to protect something unless you understand it and are intrigued by it."**

daughters' science projects along to show the students."

Pamela feels lucky to be able to combine science and writing. "Science was my first love," she says. "In school, my favourite subject was biology." She continued studying the environment in university, visiting bogs and wetlands, and observing birds and plants. She got started as a writer after working on a mosquito study in an Alberta wetland. She was asked to write a kit for schools about wetlands—and she's never looked back.

The advantage of writing non-fiction, Pamela explains, is that you do research and learn new things all the time.

Pamela's advice for young writers is: you're never too young (or too old!) to start writing. "Writing is fun, but it's also a lot of hard work. Don't get discouraged. You have to be patient. Sometimes I have to wait five years from the time I get an idea for a book until I see the book in print."

All of Pamela Hickman's books have a similar message. She wants to spread the word about special habitats—like the Atlantic seashore, forests, and wetlands—and to get people enthusiastic about protecting them.

Pamela Hickman and students on a nature walk.

BEFORE READING

High up in the mountains lies a special ecosystem—the alpine tundra. This article uses stories to introduce you to some of the animals that live there.

Above the

Article by Ann Cooper   **Pictures by Dorothy Emerling**

High in the mountains lies a treeless landscape called the alpine tundra. In summer, clear streams bubble from the glaciers and melting snowbeds. Cottony clouds scud across the sky. They cast quick shadows on the flowery meadows and fellfields. Alpine tundra is wild, full of peace and silence.

The alpine tundra can be a harsh place, too. Storms rage all winter long. Snow fluffs down to fill forests below treeline. It blankets peaks, rock slides, and fellfields. Strong winds blow feathery snow plumes off high ridges. The uncovered grasses are brown and crisp and dry. Their roots are locked in ice.

Spring comes late. In sheltered hollows, snow beds last until summer—or never melt at all. Summer is short. Plants have little time to grow. Trees at the jagged forest edge and in dotted tree islands are old, but small and twisted. They are shaped by wind and frost. Throughout the year, winds blow. Hail or snow may fall.

Treeline

Who would live in a place with little shelter, where food is often hard to find? Only crisscross tracks in a summer snow hint at stories to tell—many stories of animals that live in this harsh and lovely land.

Little Bighorn

One late spring morning, a band of bighorn ewes grazed in a meadow—all but one ewe. She felt restless. Her time had come to find a good place for a birth day. Ewe trotted away and came to a grassy hideout among crags, where no cougar or coyote could surprise her. A ledge hid her from hunting eagles soaring high above.

Ewe bleated and pawed at the ground. Her body strained. Soon her lamb was born. She licked dry Lamb's woolly coat. A few minutes later, Lamb, still wobbly, struggled to his feet, and nursed. Day after day, Ewe grazed tasty flowers and sweet grass. Lamb tagged along, nursing when hungry, resting and playing.

Ewe and Lamb stayed in their grassy hollow for about a week. By then, Lamb was strong enough to follow Ewe on a journey to rejoin her band. Safety lay in company. And company meant play! All summer, Lamb frisked, chased, and played king-of-the-rock with the other lambs, practising sheep ways.

Eagle's Day

Eagle was hunting-hungry. Wings outstretched, she circled high in the sky. Her sharp eyes scanned the meadow far below. She saw no snowshoe hares hopping among the bright wildflowers at the forest edge. Not one marmot sat on its lookout rock in the boulder field. Eagle had not scared the marmots with her shadow. It was too cloudy for that. The marmots had run underground to escape the coming storm.

Eagle needed food—for herself and for her young back in the nest. Each day her two eaglets grew larger, stronger, and hungrier. They leaped up and down on the nest and practised flapping their wings. Soon, they would fly and learn to hunt. For now, Eagle and her mate were the busy hunters.

Eagle saw a flicker of movement. A weasel! It looped in and out of the willows, nose low to a vole trail, intent on hunting. Eagle swooped down, her talons ready. Too late. Weasel heard the rush of her wings and felt a shiver of danger. Quick as a blink, Weasel whisked to safety.

Eagle flapped her wings and rose to the air again. She soared far away over the forest until she was a tiny speck against the rising storm clouds.

Links of Life

As the seasons change and years pass, many animals live out their stories above the treeline. They build homes and raise families. Young ones grow fat on the plenty of summer.

Some animals leave the high mountains before winter creeps in to lock the land in ice. Some animals sleep away the snowy season, deep in their underground homes. Other animals keep going in the worst of stormy weather.

The hunters hunt. That is the way it must be. The hunted animals run, or hide, or sometimes get caught. That is also the way it must be.

No animal lives its life apart and alone. Every animal is equally important to the way things work. Every single animal and plant that lives is a needed link in the whole pattern of nature.

What new animals did you meet in this article? Do you think that animal stories are a good way to present information? Explain your answer.

Understanding the Article

A Harsh and Lovely Land

- What animals are the natural enemies of the bighorn sheep?
- What kinds of animals are the prey of the eagle?
- Why does the author say "No animal lives its life apart and alone"?
- What are some of the "links of life" in this mountain ecosystem?
- What are some of the "links of life" in your community?

IMAGINE!

You are an artist hired to draw an alpine landscape. What will you include in your scene?

Something To Think About

The world described in this article is "wild, full of peace and silence." What kinds of people have seen this land? How do you think people should behave if they go there?

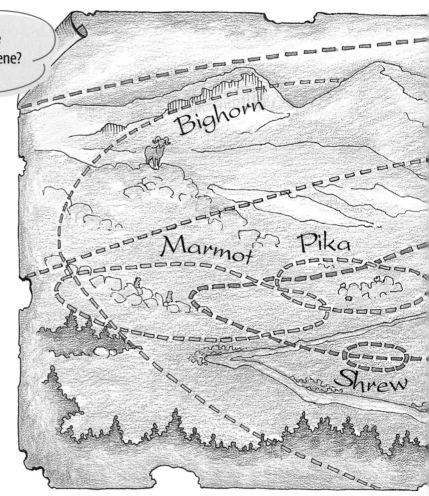

Bighorn

Marmot   Pika

Shrew

Alpine Tundra — Treeline

Look on the map below for

(a) places where high-country animals live and

(b) lines that show how much space each kind of animal needs for its home and food.

Animals do not share space equally. Some hunt over a whole mountain range. Some use only a small bit of stream and meadow.

This map gives you interesting information, but it also raises all sorts of questions. Make a list of five questions that you would like to find answers for. Begin your questions with a variety of question words:

Who? What? Where? When? Why? How?

How many?   How long?   Is it true that...?

Discuss these questions with a partner. Together, research to find answers to some of these questions. You could check non-fiction reference books, the Internet, or wildlife associations.

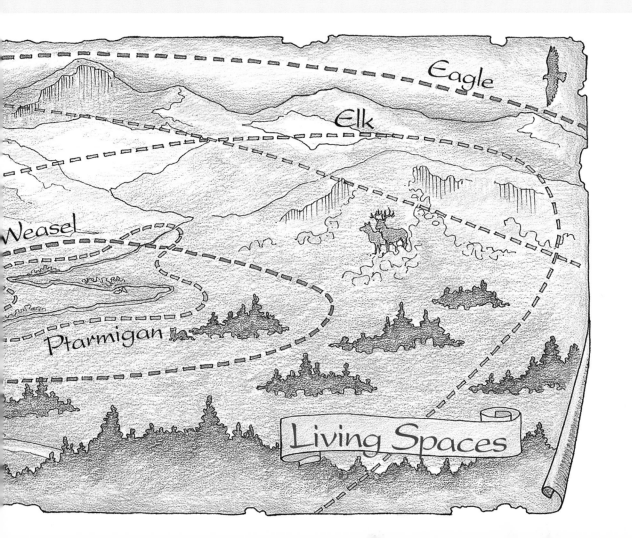

BEFORE READING

What do you think this story will be about? Consider the title, use picture clues, and recall your own experiences with a creek. Now write your predictions in your notebook.

Salmon Glossary

alevin: a very young fish

chum: a Pacific salmon, metallic blue and silver, with pink flesh

coho: a Pacific salmon, metallic blue and silver, with red flesh

redd: a hollow in the bed of a stream or creek made by the female fish, in which she lays her eggs

salmon fry: young salmon, from the time they hatch and are free-swimming

Garbage Creek

Story by W. D. Valgardson   Pictures by John Etheridge

Not wanted. That's what Jim was thinking as he kicked a can down the road. With every kick it went spinning away.

Not wanted. Not any more. Now all they could talk about was the baby this and the baby that.

His mom was always saying, "I'm too tired to read to you. Don't make so much noise. Go play quietly." The baby always needed her diapers changed. She was always eating. If she didn't eat so much, she wouldn't need her diapers changed so often.

Jim gave the can another kick. It went flying through the air, off the trail, down the slope and into the creek. He ran down after it. Stupid can, he thought.

He was surprised to see a girl sitting on a rock. He really didn't want to talk to anyone but she was holding the tin can.

"This yours?" she asked.

"Yeah," he said, taking it.

"I'm Angie. I live up there."

"Jim." He pointed back along the creek. "What're you doing?"

"Looking for arrowheads."

He looked around. It was just a little creek with a bunch of junk dumped into it. He sat down on an old tire.

"You want to go to the salt chuck?" Angie asked.

They followed the stream, hopping from rock to rock, wading in the water sometimes. The trees hung over the stream on both sides. They startled a couple of dippers that were looking for insects in the gravel bottom. When they got to the salt chuck, there was a field of grass. There were wild rose bushes and blackberry brambles. They stopped to pick blackberries. They saw a crane and some mallards.

"There used to be salmon in this creek," Angie said on the way back.

"This little thing?"

They searched for arrowheads but didn't find any. Instead they found some tin cans and bottles and plastic. They kept the drink cans and bottles and threw the rest of the garbage onto the bank.

"You're sure there's arrowheads here?" Jim said.

"I've got six at home. Two aren't so good but I've got four good ones. One's red and two are white and one is blue. There's supposed to be a midden but I haven't been able to find it."

That night the baby cried all night. It didn't fall asleep until morning. Jim made himself a peanut butter and jelly sandwich for breakfast. Then his mother chased him outside because she didn't want the baby to wake up.

"You came back," Angie said when he arrived at the creek. "I thought you said there was no point looking for arrowheads here."

"You got any brothers or sisters?"

"Four. They've all moved out. They're too busy to do anything with me."

"I'll give you my sister." Jim had brought a garden trowel. They used it to dig in the gravel and along the bank. They found clam and mussel shells. They found an animal bone that was broken on one end. Angie said that meant someone had dug out the marrow.

As they searched, they kept picking up garbage and tossing it onto the bank.

"No wonder the salmon don't come here any more. I wouldn't either," Jim said disgustedly. "Look at this." It was the rusted front wheel of a bicycle. He heaved it out of the water. "They call this Sugar Creek. I think they should call it Garbage Creek."

"How come you spend your time down here?"

"There's no place at home for me. How about you?"

"No reason. Just there's never anyone there. Me and the TV."

Jim picked up a plastic grocery bag. He started putting bits of junk in it. "You really think the Indians used to camp here? I looked up midden in the dictionary."

"My dad said my grandpa's dad used to come here in the fall to spear salmon. They'd come down in their canoes and set up camp. It's not Indians. It's Cowichan. My dad's Cowichan."

They wrestled part of an old fridge out of the water.

"You know," Jim said. "About the salmon. Do you think, I mean, if you and me got rid of the junk..."

Angie sat down on a rock. "I've been wanting to try but there's just been me and I can't move some of the big things. Two can do a lot more than one."

After that, they met every day at the stream. Every day they pulled out garbage and raked over the gravel. Sometimes they found things people had thrown into the water the night before. Jim made signs saying "No littering" and nailed them up on some sticks.

"How's your sister doing?" Angie asked one afternoon.

"Noisy. She's always crying. My mom's always changing her diapers and giving her a bottle. She wakes them up at night and then they're grouchy in the morning. What about your parents?"

"Working. My dad's a carver and he's always going places to show his carvings. My mom works for the government."

They met nearly every day for the rest of the summer. They made a trip on their bikes out to the Salmon House and watched all the movies and studied all the displays. They took the bus to the library and read books on salmon. They borrowed their parents' shovels and rakes. They saw belted kingfishers. One day they counted six eagles. As they were cleaning up the creek, they saw crayfish and diving beetles.

"Those are called water tigers," Jim said, showing Angie a diving-beetle larva.

They were still looking for arrowheads. They found some chipped flakes of rock and a stone that might have been used as a hammer. They took a couple of days off to go to Totem Pole Park and the provincial museum. They looked at the masks and sat in the longhouse.

"My dad makes masks like that," Angie said. "And pictures and stuff."

"My dad has a computer business. People are always calling with problems."

"I'm Cowichan and Scots. What about you?"

"Canadian."

"Me, too. But the other stuff. Before you got here."

"Ukrainian. Polish. My dad says my mom is the peroghi princess."

On one of their trips to the library, they stopped at the Ukrainian centre and Jim showed Angie some books written in Ukrainian. "Crazy alphabet, eh?" They went downstairs and watched some dancers practising for a concert.

"Can you speak Ukrainian?"

Jim counted on his fingers. "Six words. Can you speak Cowichan?"

Angie counted on her fingers. "Eight."

"I'll teach you six Ukrainian words if you teach me eight Cowichan."

They went back to their stream. They kept hauling out junk and raking over the gravel to get rid of the clay someone had dumped. One day they hiked to a second larger creek. It was too big and deep to cross. They stood on the bank looking at it. It was clogged with debris from logging. Garbage was caught among the branches and small logs.

"I looked this one up," Jim said. "It's called Washing Creek. It used to have salmon, too. Lots of them."

September came and it was time to go back to school. They visited their stream on weekends. But Jim had a job delivering flyers and Angie was involved in sports so they weren't able to make it every weekend.

"Hey, guy," his dad said one day. "What's so interesting about the sky? You keep looking up all the time, you'll get a crick in your neck."

"Rain clouds," Jim said. He was thinking about how the salmon would be returning soon and they needed water.

The baby had an ear infection. She'd been crying for days. That meant a trip to the doctor. Then they all went shopping for a crib. When they came out of the mall, it was raining.

After that it rained pretty regularly. On the last weekend in October, Jim met Angie at the bus stop and they took the bus out to Goldstream Park. The salmon were running. The parking lot was jammed. There were people lined up all along the river bank. Clouds of seagulls filled the air. Maple leaves as big as plates were twirling to the ground.

They walked along the river bank. They could see the backs of the chum sticking out of the water. There were lots of them. Here and there were the cherry-red backs of the coho.

"It's too crowded," Jim said.

They took the bus back. Neither one said much. They were thinking about Garbage Creek. About all the work they had done. They walked to the stream, sort of hurrying, then slowing down, like they wanted to get there but they didn't want to get there.

The rain was coming down steadily. There was 30 cm of water in the stream. They walked along the bank.

"No more fish than arrowheads," Jim said disgustedly.

"Maybe it's been too long. Maybe the fish forgot there's a stream here."

"Maybe we need to do a salmon dance."

"Don't know one."

The next day Angie took two bags out of her packsack. Carefully, she unfolded tissue paper. First she took out one mask, then another. They were carved from cedar and were painted in bright colours. One was a salmon mask. The other was of a beaver.

"These are mine," she said. "I've got eagle and killer whale, too, but I thought they'd frighten the salmon. Maybe if we wear these, the fish will remember. Maybe the stream will look like it did a long time ago."

They went to where the stream and the salt marsh met. They sat side by side in the tall grass and held the masks over their faces.

Suddenly, Angie grabbed Jim's arm. She put her finger to her lips, then pointed.

There, just inside the entrance, hiding under the overhanging bank, were two coho, their tails slowly moving back and forth. Cautiously, the fish edged into the stream. They moved forward, then let the current push them back. In a sudden burst the female made a dash forward. The male followed. Then the female stopped, turned on her side and began to beat the gravel violently with her tail.

"She's making a redd," Jim whispered excitedly.

The female kept beating at the gravel until there was a small depression. She tested the depth with her tail. She lay over it and they could see her laying the eggs. Then the male swam forward to fertilize the eggs. The female rushed ahead and began to make a new nest.

Angie and Jim watched for hours. The female's tail gradually became tattered. Both fish lay still in the current.

"They're tired," Angie said. "All that work to make a nest and have some babies."

Angie and Jim came back to the stream the next day and the next. Gradually, the two fish became covered in white blotches. On the third day, both fish were floating in an eddy.

"It's not fair," Angie said.

"No." Jim was sitting on a rock. He'd got so he thought of the two salmon as his salmon. "Lots of things aren't fair. They just are."

During the winter, because they went to different schools and were busy with homework and sports and clubs, they only got to meet at the creek occasionally. The trees had shed their leaves. The water looked cold.

One Friday Jim called Angie and asked her to meet him at the creek. He felt sort of shy. They hadn't seen each other for awhile. They both said hello. They asked each other about school.

"How're things going at home?" Angie asked.

"Okay, I guess. She's crawling around and she can just about say something. She wants to climb on top of me when I'm lying on the floor watching TV. I'm helping her learn to walk. How about you?"

"My oldest brother took me to a rock concert in Vancouver."

"The eggs should be hatching now," Jim said. "I wrote it on my calendar." He took out a pamphlet he had got on salmon. They searched but couldn't find anything.

"They're too little," Angie said. "They're still alevins. They're hiding under the gravel. We've got to wait until April."

Jim checked the creek every couple of weeks. He saw a mink and a deer and a number of cranes but no salmon fry.

Then, the first week in April, Angie called him. They met at the creek on a Saturday morning.

They were standing in the water, peering down. All at once, Jim shouted, "Look! There they are."

Salmon fry scattered through the water.

Jim laughed. "We're parents." He felt embarrassed. "I mean...you know what I mean."

"Grandparents. Next year we'll be great-grandparents."

There weren't a lot of fry. But there were some. Jim and Angie looked up and down the stream. Someone had thrown some paper cups into it in spite of the signs. They picked them up and put them in a garbage bag.

They crouched down to watch the fry dart about.

"Ours," Angie said. "We did it. They wouldn't be here if it weren't for us."

Jim nodded and grinned. "We never found any arrowheads though."

Angie reached into her pocket. "Put your hand out," she said. "I brought you something." She took her hand out of her pocket, then held it over his. She put something in his hand. It was her blue arrowhead.

He put his hand in his pocket. He took out a wooden doll. He turned the top. It came apart. Inside was another little doll. He opened this one and there was another doll inside.
"I brought you something, too," he said and gave it to her.
"To celebrate."

They both looked at the water. Here and there they could see the fry darting back and forth.

"We've still got work to do," Angie said. "They're going to be here for a year before they go to sea. You and me, we're going to have to keep Sugar Creek clean for them. And maybe even another pair will turn up in the fall."

"Being a parent is hard work," Jim said, laughing. He looked at Angie. Maybe, he thought, if his sister turned out like Angie, it wouldn't be so bad having her around after all.

Choose a partner and discuss your predictions. Did the story match your predictions? What surprises did the story hold?

STORY STRUCTURE

Three-Part Stories

Many stories can be divided into three basic parts.

Part 1, The Set-Up: In this part, the author introduces the main characters and explains what they want to do.

Part 2, Problems: In this part, usually the longest part, the characters face problems. The problems get in the way of what they want to do.

Part 3, The Solution: Finally, the characters solve their problems. Often, they have grown and changed through their experiences.

With three or four classmates, discuss how *Garbage Creek* follows this story structure. Think of titles to describe each section of the story.

Understanding the Story

Watching a Friendship Grow

- At the beginning of the story, Jim and Angie feel the same way. What are their feelings, and why do they feel this way?
- Why do they start cleaning up the creek together?
- What methods do they use to locate information about salmon?

- By the end, how have Jim and Angie's feelings about their families—and each other—changed? Why do their feelings change?
- Do you predict that their friendship will continue? Explain your answer.

A Story

Do you have interesting memories about yourself and nature? Brainstorm as many ideas as you can about feelings or adventures you've had in a forest, on a lake, on a mountain, or wherever you like! Then plan a story based on one of your memories.

First make an outline based on the three-part story structure.

1. The Set-up
2. The Problem(s)
3. The Solution

Next, write a first draft. Ask a partner to read it and make helpful comments. Then make revisions.

Finally, when you are pleased with the story, write it out neatly or publish it using a computer. Add illustrations or photos and share your story with your classmates or family. Ask them for feedback.

IMAGINE!

You're a famous wood carver. Design a mask based on your favourite animal, bird or fish.

Find Out More About...

The story *Garbage Creek* tells you quite a lot about salmon. We learn that Pacific salmon spawn (produce eggs) in creeks and rivers in British Columbia. But there is much more to find out about their complete life cycle. Find some good books about salmon in the library. Use illustrations to show the life cycle of salmon (Atlantic or Pacific salmon) and share this information with your classmates.

The Web of Life

POEM BY **Nancy Wood**   PICTURE BY **Daphne McCormick**

To kill the owl
   is to kill
   the mountains in their majesty.
To kill the bear
   is to kill
   the beauty of all living things.
The web of life
   connects grass to fish
   trees to turtles
   sky to caterpillars.
The web of life
   connects me to everything
   that came before,
   even to the moment
   when earth herself was born.
To break the web of life
   is to fill the universe
   with pain.

Personal Response

- What does poet Nancy Wood mean by "the web of life"? Do you agree with her ideas?
- When animals kill each other for food, are they breaking the web of life?
- What are some of the ways that people break the web of life?
- What are some things you can do to keep the web of life strong?

Create Your Own Web of Life

Make a list of the living creatures who are part of your personal web of life. Include all the plants, animals, and people that matter to you. How are you connected to each of them?

Design an illustrated web called "My Web of Life." Share your web with others.

MORE GOOD READING

In the Heart of the Village
by Barbara Bash

One old banyan tree is a forest habitat in itself, home to nesting birds, flying monkeys, and happy children. (an informational picture book)

Oceans
by Adrienne Mason

Get acquainted with some amazing coral reefs, sea mammals, fish, and seaweed through this book and its photos. (a science book)

Habitats
by Pamela Hickman

This book shows you how to set up and care for different mini-habitats—such as worms in a jar, or toads in a terrarium. (a how-to science book)

Voices from the Wild
by Dave Bouchard

In these 25 poems and paintings each animal explains how it uses its senses. The grizzly, for example, relies on his acute sense of smell as he roams his mountain territory. (a poetry collection)

How Monkeys Make Chocolate **by Adrian Forsyth**

Did you know that monkeys make chocolate? Or that poison from the eyelash viper snake can be used to make medicine for blood pressure? Explore these and other mysteries of the tropical rainforest. (a science book)

HEROES
Old and
New

A Song of Greatness

A Chippewa Song,
translated by Mary Austin

When I hear the old men
Telling of heroes,
Telling of great deeds
Of ancient days,
When I hear them telling,
Then I think within me
I too am one of these.

When I hear the people
Praising great ones,
Then I know that I too
Shall be esteemed,
I too when my time comes
Shall do mightily.

Who is your personal hero? Here are some answers from kids just like you.

My Hero Is...

Personal Anecdotes by Canadian Children
Pictures by Philippe Béha

My dog is my hero. He looks scruffy, but his brains work because one day he barked and woke us up. That saved us from a fire, and maybe death. We all got out, and we love our dog more than ever.

Anna, age 11

My hero is my little brother Jamin. He has muscular dystrophy and until he was eight he could walk around mostly by himself. Now he needs a wheelchair. My brother keeps a good attitude and doesn't complain. He keeps me happy.

Tomaru, age 11

My hero is my teacher because she listens to me. She's an artist and I want to be one when I grow up. She teaches me at recess and after school.

Davian, age 11

FOLLOW UP

Did any of the students choose the same kind of hero as you did? Were their reasons similar or different? Did any of their heroes surprise you?

What Is a Hero?

CLASS DISCUSSION

- Make a chalkboard list of the qualities these student writers admire in their personal heroes.

- Next, imagine you are on a committee that gives out awards for heroism (for example, to someone who has saved a child from drowning). Make a list of the qualities your committee is looking for.

- Now, make a list of famous heroes in the news, or from books or movies. List the qualities these heroes have.

- Finally, compare these lists. What quality or characteristic do you think it is most important for heroes to have?

My hero is my mom. We have seven kids in our family and Mom spends time with all of us. That's important because our dad died and she's all alone. My mom takes extra jobs at home, and makes money that way. It must be hard to be in charge of so many kids.

Theresa, age 11

Portrait of a Hero

YOUR TURN TO WRITE

A portrait can be a picture in words. Write a short portrait about your personal hero. Describe the qualities and characteristics of your hero and then explain why the person (or animal) is a hero to you. When you have polished your portrait, you could add a photograph or illustration. Add your portrait to a class display of heroes.

BEFORE READING

Preview the article by reading the titles, headings, and type in boxes. Now, think about how you would define a super hero. As you read the article, decide who's the greatest super hero.

Article by
CLAIRE WATTS
and
ROBERT NICHOLSON

SUPER

Thor

The Norse god of thunder, Thor, got into frequent fights with giants. One of them was Skrymir, a frost giant so big that Thor slept in the thumb of his empty glove thinking he was inside a house!

LEGENDARY SUPER HEROES

Picture the scene: the world is threatened by terrible danger at the hands of some dastardly villain. Time is running out. Is there anyone who can save the day? We need someone strong, someone fearless—we need a hero!

This isn't just the plot of an action-packed film, it's a story that's been told again and again—ever since people first began to entertain each other with amazing stories.

HEROES

Often they started as tales about real people but, as the stories were passed from one person to another, they became more and more exaggerated. A fight against three people became a battle against ten and then one hundred fearsome enemies. A favourite weapon became an invincible magic tool.

Most legendary heroes have some kind of superhuman powers. The heroes of ancient Greek legends are usually related to the gods. This means they are extra strong, extra clever, and always have luck on their side. The best known of them, Hercules, was only a baby when he strangled two snakes sent to kill him.

MAGIC POWERS

Some heroes are also helped by magic. Odin, the Vikings' most important god, had an invincible spear called *Gungnir*. He also had two ravens which perched on his shoulders and flew off to spy on his enemies. Odin's son, Thor, had a hammer called *Mjolnir* ("the destroyer"), which returned like a boomerang whenever he

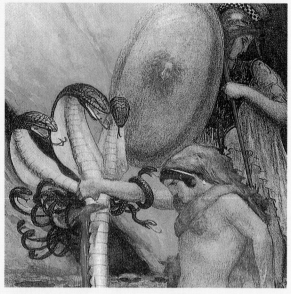

Hercules

Hercules is famous for the 12 tasks, or "labours," set for him by King Eurystheus of Tiryns. These included killing monsters, cleaning a stable by diverting a river, and taming a herd of man-eating horses. He proved his amazing strength many times, once even holding up the sky in place of the giant Atlas.

threw it. He also had a magic belt that doubled his strength.

But not all heroes have superhuman skills or magic powers. Some have only their own wits to rely on. Odysseus, for example, captured the city of Troy by hiding his Greek army inside a huge wooden horse. The Trojans thought it was a gift from the Greeks—but they got an unpleasant surprise when Odysseus's men jumped out!

FATAL FLAW

Few heroes are totally invincible, though. Most have one weakness that can destroy them.

In the case of Achilles, the great Greek warrior of the Trojan War, it was his heel. When he was a baby, his mother dipped him in the magic River Styx, which made his whole body invulnerable—except the heel by which he was held. He was finally killed when a poisoned arrow struck him on it. That's why someone's weak point is often known as an "Achilles heel."

Boadicea

Legends soon grow up about real people who act in extraordinary or brave ways. In A.D. 60 Boadicea (or Boudicca), the queen of a British people called the Iceni, led a rebellion against Roman invaders. Her army defeated the Roman troops three times before being overcome in A.D. 61. It didn't take long before legendary tales of this courageous queen were being passed on.

Atalanta

Atalanta was a Greek princess who was raised by bears. The bears, and later Artemis, the goddess of hunting, taught Atalanta to be a great hunter. Atalanta could run faster than anyone in Greece. She was famous for her swiftness, her bravery in fighting centaurs and monsters, and her skill in hunting and fishing.

Brave Warriors

Some other heroic females include the Amazons, Gulnara, and Joan of Arc.

The Amazons are strong, brave, and fierce warriors of Greek legends. The Ancient Greeks told many stories about the Amazons. One tale tells how Hercules fought Hippolyta, a famous Amazon queen.

Gulnara, a young Mongolian girl, boldly took her father's place as a soldier in the army. Her courage and wisdom brought peace to her land.

Joan of Arc was a young French woman. At the age of seventeen she bravely led an army to victory against English invaders.

COMIC BOOK SUPER HEROES

COMIC BOOK SUPER HEROES
How do these modern super heroes measure up to the legendary heroes?

Superman is from the planet Krypton. He came to Earth as a baby in a spaceship, just before his planet was destroyed by a huge explosion. His foster parents on Earth were Jonathan and Martha Kent, who named him Clark. Whenever his superpowers are needed, Clark races to the nearest phone box and emerges as Superman—ready to fly into battle with criminals everywhere.

Batman is really millionaire Bruce Wayne. When he was a boy, Bruce saw a mugger kill his parents—and from then on, he swore to devote his life to fighting crime. His Batman disguise strikes terror into the hearts of cowardly criminals. Whenever Gotham City is overrun by crime, Police Commissioner Gordon calls up Batman by shining a giant bat-signal high into the night sky.

	Superman	Batman
Secret identity	Mild-mannered reporter Clark Kent	Millionaire Bruce Wayne
Nicknames	Man of Steel, Man of Tomorrow	The Caped Crusader, the Masked Manhunter
Uniform	Blue tights and shirt, has a yellow logo with a red **S** in the middle of it; red trunks, cape, and long boots	Dark grey cape with blue mask and hood, black-and-yellow bat logo on chest (In the most recent films, Batman has favoured a sinister black mask.)
Superpowers	X-ray vision, ability to fly, incredible strength, faster than a speeding bullet	Equipment belt with grappling hooks to scale buildings, nerve gas, freezing compound
City	Metropolis	Gotham City
Enemy no. 1	Lex Luthor, super-criminal supreme	The Joker
Other enemies	Terra-Man, Brainiac, Mr. Mxyzptlk, Nuclear Man, Spider Lady	The Penguin, The Riddler, Catwoman, Two-Face
Partners	Supergirl, Lois Lane	Robin the Boy Wonder, Alfred the butler, Batgirl
Hero History	*Superman* was invented by two teenagers, Jerry Siegel and Joe Schuster, a Canadian. (In fact, Metropolis is modelled after Toronto of the 1930s). They first came up with the idea back in 1933. But it wasn't until June 1938 that the Man of Steel made his first appearance in *Action Comics No. 1*.	*Batman* was created by artist Bob Kane and writer Bill Finger in 1939. His first appearance was in *Detective Comics No. 27* in May 1939 and he soon came up against an awesome array of fearful foes.

INDESTRUCTIBLE
Superman can only be killed by a green stone called Kryptonite, the fragment remains of the planet Krypton.

MORE COMIC SUPER HEROES

Wonder Woman

Diana Prince, also known as *Wonder Woman*, first appeared in a comic in 1941. She's an Amazon warrior (like Xena) whose armour includes a lasso of truth and bullet-deflecting bracelets. With these to aid her, she defends the innocent from villains.

Spider-Man

Skinny schoolboy Peter Parker was bitten by a radioactive spider and developed incredible superpowers. As *Spider-Man,* he spins webs strong enough to climb up skyscrapers and ensnare his villainous enemies.

Captain Marvel

Captain Marvel was born when paperboy Billy Batson uttered the magic word *Shazam* and gained

- the wisdom of Solomon
- the strength of Hercules
- the stamina of Atlas
- the power of Zeus
- the courage of Achilles
- and the speed of Mercury.

Red Raven

Red Raven is a super hero created by Charles Fiddler of The Pas, Manitoba. In the first issue, the courageous *Oske-pi'sew* (the Cree word for Lynx) tries to protect his people from a crazed bear, and is knocked out. An evil sorcerer, the person behind the bear's attack, then turns the villagers to ice statues. When Oske-pi'sew wakes he finds out what has happened from an old shaman. The shaman tells Oske-pi'sew he can save his people by getting the star-stone, which is protected by a red raven, a magical creature. When Oske-pi'sew accidentally kills the raven and picks up the stone he *becomes* the Red Raven, a creature with super powers. With these powers he is able to fight the sorcerer and save his people.

FOLLOW UP

Who do you think is the greatest super hero in the article? Do you have a favourite super hero who wasn't mentioned? Share your choice of super hero with a partner.

 Create a Super Hero Display

Every culture has its own legendary heroes. Ask family members to retell any stories they know, or check the library to find out about heroes from other cultures. Make a classroom display of heroes from around the world.

 TECH LINK
You could use a database to collect and organize your information.

Understanding the Selection

It's a Bird, It's a Plane, It's...!

- Stories about legendary heroes (on pages 100 to 102) have been told for thousands of years. How do the stories become exaggerated as time goes by?

- List three legendary heroes and the superhuman powers they use to help them in their heroic deeds.

- Modern comic book heroes have a lot in common with legendary heroes. With a partner discuss
  (a) the superhuman powers of one modern hero and one legendary hero,
  (b) the enemies they fight against.

IMAGINE!
Captain Marvel had a magic word created from the initials of other words. Use the same method to make up your own powerful magic word!

A Super Hero Tale

Create a new super hero, female or male. Begin by filling in a chart, like the ones for Superman and Batman, giving your hero a name and characteristics. Draw pictures of your hero in action. Then outline a story in which your hero uses superhuman powers to defeat an enemy. Finally, shape your story into a comic book!

Super Heroes Hit the Screen

Create a list of movies and TV shows, old and new, about legendary super heroes and comic book super heroes. Select a few to watch. Decide which of the shows is most successful. In your notebook, fill in a chart like this for one or two shows.

Name of Show ____	Yes	No	Examples
☆ The super hero is both powerful and likable.	—	—	____
☆ The deeds she or he performs are truly amazing.	—	—	____
☆ The animation or special effects are terrific.	—	—	____
☆ The show keeps you on the edge of your seat with excitement.	—	—	____
☆ There are moments of humour or romance.	—	—	____

Something To Think About!

Why are there more male than female super heroes? Is this fair? Are things changing? Discuss this with a small group.

Lucy Lawless as Xena, Warrior Princess

Shaquille O'Neal as John Henry Irons-Steel

BEFORE READING

This ancient Greek legend tells how a young man is tested to find out if he's a true hero. Read on to discover what the test is, and whether he passes.

Bellerophon

AND THE
Flying Horse

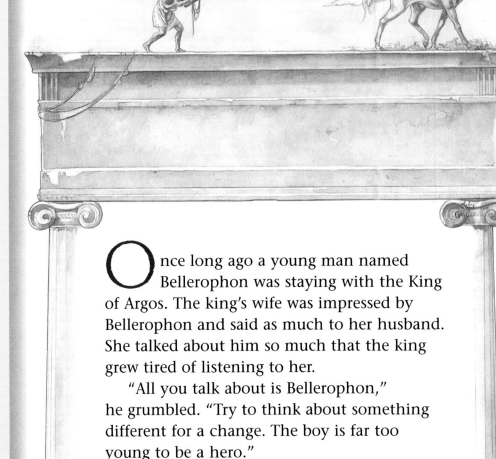

GREEK LEGEND
RETOLD BY
Pamela Oldfield

PICTURES BY
Nick Harris

PRONUNCIATION GUIDE

Argos: AR-gos

Athena: Ah-THEEN-ah

Bellerophon:
Bel-ER-oh-fon

Chimera: Ky-MEER-ah
(ky as in "sky")

Lycia: LISH-ah

Pegasus: PEG-ah-sus

Once long ago a young man named Bellerophon was staying with the King of Argos. The king's wife was impressed by Bellerophon and said as much to her husband. She talked about him so much that the king grew tired of listening to her.

"All you talk about is Bellerophon," he grumbled. "Try to think about something different for a change. The boy is far too young to be a hero."

His wife took no notice. Day after day she told the king how handsome Bellerophon was, how clever and how brave. At last the king grew so jealous that he decided to get rid of Bellerophon, but without telling his wife.

He handed Bellerophon a sealed letter and asked him to deliver it to the King of Lycia.

"This is a most important letter," he told Bellerophon. "Be sure you give it to him."

Bellerophon agreed to deliver the letter and set off at once. He soon reached Lycia and met the king. The two of them got on well right from the start. The king entertained him so lavishly that it was several days before Bellerophon remembered the letter.

"Forgive me, Your Majesty," he said. "I was asked to give you this." The king opened the letter. As he read it he turned quite pale.

"Whatever is the matter?" asked Bellerophon. "Is it bad news?" The king made no answer, but began to mutter to himself.

"This is treachery," he whispered. "I cannot believe it." Then he looked up at Bellerophon. "Never ask me about this letter," he commanded, and he threw it straight on the fire.

That night when Bellerophon went to bed he wondered about what was in the letter, but he was tired and soon fell asleep. The king, however, could not sleep. The letter had given him a terrible shock. It said that Bellerophon was a wicked young man and asked the king to have him killed.

"How could I do such a thing?" murmured the king. "Bellerophon seems such a pleasant young man, and he is a guest in my house. The King of Argos is known for his hot temper and he may soon regret this rash decision."

He paced up and down until at last he had an idea. "I shall send Bellerophon to slay the Chimera," he decided. "He may well die in the attempt, but if he succeeds even the King of Argos will have to admit that he is a true hero."

So the next day the king told Bellerophon about the ferocious monster that was causing distress to the people of his kingdom, and begged him to do something about it.

"The Chimera is ruining their lives," said the king. "I implore you to destroy it for me. You will find it over in the hills where the sun rises."

Bellerophon was rather puzzled by all this, but he agreed to go. He walked for many kilometres without seeing a sign of the monster and eventually stopped to ask an old farmer if he was going in the right direction. When Bellerophon mentioned what he was looking for, the old man's eyes widened in alarm.

"Stay away from the Chimera," he warned Bellerophon. "It's the vilest creature ever born. Plenty of young men have tried to kill it, but they have all died in the attempt."

"Perhaps I will have better luck," said Bellerophon hopefully. The old farmer shook his head.

"Young people today just will not listen to reason," he grumbled, "but if you are determined to get yourself killed, take that path through the woods. It will lead you to the Chimera."

Bellerophon thanked the farmer politely and went on his way, trying not to be alarmed by what he had been told. He was not looking forward to fighting the Chimera, but if he turned back without even trying he would be called a coward.

An hour later he sat down to rest, and to his astonishment a beautiful woman appeared before him.

"I am Athena, goddess of wisdom," she told him. "I know you plan to fight the Chimera and I will help you." She held out a bridle, and as Bellerophon took it from her she smiled at him and vanished.

"How odd," thought Bellerophon, staring at the bridle. "What possible use could a bridle be when I have no horse?" The bridle was of finest white leather studded with gold and decorated with precious jewels. "I shall take it with me," he said, and went on his way, puzzling over the strange gift.

What Bellerophon did not notice was that far above him Pegasus, the winged horse of the gods, was wheeling and prancing among the clouds. Suddenly the snow-white horse flew down to earth to drink at a spring of pure water. Bellerophon was overjoyed when he saw the graceful creature before him. Now he knew why Athena had given him the bridle.

He approached the horse slowly, speaking softly to reassure him. "I know you are Pegasus," he said. "You are always ridden by the gods. I am not a god, but Athena has given me this bridle and I must ride you when I go to fight the dreadful Chimera." Pegasus nodded his head as if he understood, but just as Bellerophon reached out to touch him, the horse sprang into the air and out of reach. For a moment Bellerophon thought the horse would fly away, but then he came down again to drink. Eventually Bellerophon gave up his attempt to catch the horse. He put down the bridle and stood by, quietly observing. Pegasus was a fine animal with hoofs and wings of silver and a flowing mane and tail. Suddenly Bellerophon ran forward, jumped onto the horse's back, and clung to its mane. The horse tried every trick he knew to throw off his unwanted rider. He flew up into the air and swooped down again, but somehow Bellerophon managed to stay on its back. At last Pegasus flew down to land beside the spring once more.

Bellerophon guessed that now Pegasus would wear the bridle and he slipped it over the horse's head. Then he sprang once more onto the horse's back. "Take me to the Chimera!" he cried and Pegasus leaped upward, tossing his head with excitement.

They flew for many kilometres until at last they came to a valley where the grass and trees were trampled and broken. Far below them a village lay in ruins. From the dark hills beyond the valley they heard a thunderous rumbling roar.

"That must be the Chimera," whispered Bellerophon. He leaned forward and reassuringly patted the horse's neck, but his own heart beat faster at the thought of what was to come. Pegasus showed no fear, but flew on toward the rumbling sound. Soon they were confronted by a horrible sight. The Chimera rose up before them...this was no ordinary beast—the monster had three heads!

One head roared—it was the head of a lion. The second head hissed—it was the head of a giant snake. The third and last head bleated like a goat and had two sharp horns.

Bellerophon was terrified. He almost wished he could turn back, but then he remembered Athena. She had sent Pegasus to help Bellerophon and that made him feel much braver.

"Death to the cruel Chimera!" he shouted, and drew out his sword. The lion's head reached out toward him, its mouth ready to swallow him up, but the winged horse darted sideways and Bellerophon cut off the head with one mighty blow.
The Chimera's rage was frightful. The snake's head lunged at Bellerophon, hissing loudly, but down came the sword again. Chop! And away rolled the snake's head.

"Two heads gone and one to go!" shouted Bellerophon, but the Chimera was not going to be beaten quite so easily. Without warning it reared up on its hind legs and reached out with its fearsome claws. They sank into the winged horse, who whinnied with pain. Silver feathers floated down and the beautiful white mane was suddenly speckled with blood.

The sight of the horse's blood made Bellerophon forget his own fear. Without a thought for his own safety he slashed again and again at the goat's head until that too lay bleeding on the ground. Now the Chimera had lost all three of its heads, and it collapsed in a heap.

Bellerophon waited, his sword at the ready, but the Chimera would rise no more.

A great cry went up as the people ran from their hiding places in the ruined village. "The Chimera is dead!" they cried, cheering and waving as Pegasus and Bellerophon flew skyward once more. They watched the young man and the horse as they rose higher and higher and disappeared at last among the rolling clouds.

The grateful people then set about rebuilding their village and replanting their crops. The memory of the beautiful white horse and its valiant rider would live on in their hearts forever. Bellerophon had escaped death, and no one could now doubt that he was indeed a hero. ◆

FOLLOW UP

Did Bellerophon prove to be a true hero? Why or why not? Discuss your answer with a partner.

Understanding the Legend

Testing a Hero

- Why does the King of Argos want to get rid of Bellerophon? If you were the King of Argos what would you have done?

- Why does the King of Lycia want to test Bellerophon?

- How does Athena, the goddess of wisdom, help Bellerophon? Why do you think she helps him?

- What do you think Bellerophon, the new hero, will do with the rest of his life?

Storytelling

You can gain a better understanding of a story by retelling it in your own words. Here are some steps to follow as you retell *Bellerophon and the Flying Horse*.

STEP 1: Reread the story and pick out at least six key points.

STEP 2: Make rough drawings of those key points.

STEP 3: Share your drawings with a small group. Tell them the events you have portrayed. Listen as each member does the same.

STEP 4: In turn, everyone in your group should retell the whole story without using the drawings.

STEP 5: When you are feeling confident and have rehearsed many times, retell the story of Bellerophon to a family member or a group of younger students.

What Is a True Hero?

GROUP DISCUSSION

With three or four classmates, discuss the qualities of a true hero.

1. List all the heroic qualities Bellerophon shows.
2. Discuss the differences between immortals (gods, goddesses, special creatures) and mortals (human beings).
3. List the kinds of help Bellerophon received from immortal beings.
4. Decide whether or not Bellerophon could have slayed the monster all on his own.
5. Make a list of all the qualities your group thinks a true hero needs. Choose one person to present your list, with explanations, to the class.

Something To Think About!

The old farmer tells Bellerophon: "Young people today just will not listen to reason." Have you heard this remark too? Is it true today? Do you think it was true in Bellerophon's time?

IMAGINE!
You're a queen or king, and a young woman comes to you claiming to be a hero. How will you test her true heroism?

BEFORE READING

●

This Ancient Inca legend tells how a young girl proves her courage. As you read, compare her heroic deeds with Bellerophon's.

A Legend from Ecuador by HEATHER FOREST

Pictures by SUE TODD

Pronunciation Guide

Pachacuti: patch-ah-COO-tee

THE Search FOR THE Magic Lake

Long ago, a powerful Inca ruler named Pachacuti governed a vast empire in Ecuador. His palace walls were covered with gold and glistened like the sun. But his mood was always dark and sorrowful. His only son, Topa, lay weak and dying. None of the court doctors could cure him. The Inca ruler grieved and went to the altar to pray. An eerie voice drifted out to him from the flames at the altar. "Your son must drink the waters of the Magic Lake that touches the sky," it said. "Fill the magic golden flask!"

The fire smoldered to embers and when it cooled, the golden flask was lying in the ashes.

Pachacuti was too old to travel to the end of the world to fill the flask with water from the Magic Lake. He announced, "I will give a great fortune to anyone who can bring water from the Magic Lake to the palace."

Two young men who lived on a farm in the valley heard about the reward. "Let us search for the Magic Lake," they said to each other. "If we find its healing waters, we will save our Prince, and help our poor parents to live a comfortable life."

Their younger sister pleaded, "Let me come too!"

"No, stay here with our old parents," they said. "The journey will be too long and dangerous for you. We will return in time for the harvest."

Leaving their disappointed sister behind, the young men went in search of the Magic Lake. They travelled for months and still did not reach the end of the world, where the Magic Lake touches the sky.

"It is almost harvest time," said one son wearily. "Let us bring some water from any lake we find along the way and go home. Surely the Emperor will reward us for our troubles."

The two young men delivered jars of ordinary water to the palace. Doctors brought the water to the Prince. He sipped the water, but lay as pale and weak as ever.

"This water could not be from the Magic Lake," said the court doctor. "They have lied about where they found it!"

The Emperor was furious at the deception. "Lying is a serious crime. Put these men in prison!" he cried. The two were dragged away and locked in a dungeon.

When news of their imprisonment reached home, their sister said, "I will seek the Magic Lake. Perhaps, if I find it, my brothers will be freed." She filled a small sack with roasted corn and brought a bottle of chicha, a corn mash drink. With her pet llama for company, she bravely set off.

They travelled a long way down the highway. By nightfall, the girl heard the sound of a hungry puma. Trembling with fright, she said, "Go home, dear llama, where you will be safe." She chased him back down the road. For safety, she climbed a tree. Nestled in the branches, she opened her bag of roasted corn. Three small birds landed beside her on the branch. Opening her hand, she let the birds peck the corn from her palm until they had eaten most of it. She drank her chicha and fell asleep.

As she slept, one bird said, "She will never reach the Magic Lake without some help."

Another added, "She fed us, so we should help her!"

When the girl heard these small voices, she opened her eyes. The birds fluttered to a branch in front of her face. "Take a feather from each of our wings. Make them into a fan and they will help you on your way."

Then each bird plucked a downy feather from under its wing. Taking the feathers from the beaks, she made a fan and tied it at the bottom with her hair ribbon.

"I wish I were at the Magic Lake," she sighed. Instantly a strong wind arose and whisked her out of the tree. She soared over the forest and gently landed in front of a lake so large its distant shore seemed to touch the sky.

"This must be the Magic Lake!" she cried. "I wish I had a jar that could carry the healing water."

No sooner did she say these words than a golden flask landed at her feet. Just as she leaned down to pick it up, she heard something scratching the sand behind her. She turned and saw an enormous, hairy-legged crab. "Leave the water alone!" it said.

The girl held the feather fan up to her mouth and the giant crab fell asleep.

She heard a great splash in the water and turned to see a giant alligator thrust his tail against the surface. "Leave the water alone!" it said.

She held up the fan and the alligator fell asleep and floated away.

Above her there was a strong wind. She looked up to see a huge winged serpent hissing, "SSSStay away! Leave the water alone!"

She held up her feather fan to her lips and the serpent descended onto the shoreline and fell asleep too.

As quickly as she could, she filled the golden flask. "I wish I were in the palace," she said.

When she blinked again, she was standing beside the sickly Prince, ashen pale on his bed. His father and mother wept over the lifeless body of their only son.

"I have brought the healing water of the Magic Lake," said the girl, holding up the golden flask.

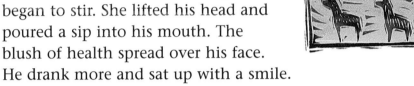

She rushed to the Prince's side and let several drops moisten his lips. He began to stir. She lifted his head and poured a sip into his mouth. The blush of health spread over his face. He drank more and sat up with a smile.

"You have saved our son!" cried the Emperor Pachacuti. "Name anything you want as a reward."

"I desire only three things," said the girl. "First, I want my parents to have a comfortable farm and a herd of llamas, vicuñas, and alpacas."

"Done!" said the Emperor.

"Next," she said, "I want you to free my brothers. Surely they have learned their lesson and will never lie again. They were trying to help my parents."

"Done!" said the Emperor.

"Lastly," she said, "I want these feathers returned to the birds who gave them to me. My mission is finished."

Before the Emperor could speak, the feather fan rose up out of her hand. It floated across the room and vanished out the window.

"What can we give you for yourself?" asked the Emperor. "Please stay here with us and live in great riches."

"No," said the girl, "my greatest reward will be to see my family together again."

She returned home to discover that royal workers were already building a new house. Her parents rejoiced and her two brothers offered humble thanks as they lifted her high up onto their shoulders and danced about the farm. 🔶

What do you think was the most important difference between this young girl and Bellerophon?

Understanding the Selection

Honest and Kind

- Why does the young girl want to go with her brothers? Why won't they let her? Do you think this is fair? Explain your answer.

- All the young girl wants as a reward is to help others. Why doesn't she want anything for herself? What would you have asked for if you had saved the Prince's life?

- What do you think is the moral of this story?

- Why do you think the author has chosen to give names only to the Emperor and his son? What would you call the brave young girl? What would you call her brothers?

Find Out More About...

With a partner, find out more about the ancient Incas, and their way of life. One of the things you might find out in your research is that young girls and boys weren't given permanent names until after their initiation at age fourteen.

TECH LINK
Use the Internet to help you in your research.

IMAGINE!

Are there any "monsters" for heroes to fight nowadays? Draw a picture of a monster for today—or for the future!

Did You Know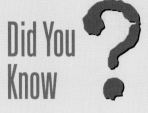

Pachacuti was the ninth Inca Emperor, in the fifth century when the Inca empire was vast, extending along the western coast of South America.

Heroes on TV

With three or four classmates, brainstorm a list of television shows with strong, courageous heroes like the young Inca girl or Bellerophon. Are the heroes we see on television today different from the legendary heroes of long ago? If so, in what ways?

Descendants of the Incas live today in many of the same ways as their ancestors did.

Comparing Heroes

In your notebook, fill in a chart like this one to compare the two heroes—Bellerophon and the young girl.

Legendary Heroes

	Bellerophon	Young Girl
Costume		
Task to Perform		
Supernatural Helper		
Type of Monster		
Magic Weapon		
Greatest Achievement		

Brave New Heights

Poem by MONICA KULLING
Picture by CHUM McLEOD

I hear Amelia Earhart
took a plane
and flew it like a bullet
straight up through clouds
into an atmosphere
we can't see

and when the engine
cut
(the plane being pushed
as high as it would go)

I hear Amelia Earhart
turned that plane
straight back
down into a blanket
of foggy cloud lying thick
and nearly to the ground

only with the clouds gone
could she pull back on the stick
the ground screaming in her face
Amelia tacked that plane
back into the sky
saving herself and breaking
another flying record

RESPONDING
to BRAVE NEW HEIGHTS

What's Happening?

CLASS DISCUSSION

What is Amelia Earhart doing in this poem? Brainstorm ideas with your classmates, writing notes on the chalkboard. When you have a clear idea of this exciting moment, develop a diagram or pictures to show what is happening in the poem.

Did You Know?

Amelia Earhart was born in Kansas, on July 24, 1898. During World War I, she worked as a military nurse in Canada. Despite her family's disapproval, she learned to fly and became famous as an aviation pioneer. In 1928, she was the first woman to cross the Atlantic—as a passenger. Four years later, this time as the pilot, she made a solo Atlantic crossing. In 1935, she crossed the Pacific alone from Hawaii to California. Then in 1937, with Fred Noonan, she attempted a round-the-world trip in a twin-engined Lockheed. They travelled two-thirds of the distance safely, but the plane vanished in the South Pacific on July 2. The exact spot has never been found.

Something To Think About!

A song from the Olympic Games begins, "Higher, stronger, faster…" Does this describe Amelia Earhart? Do you think she was a risk-taker (took unnecessary risks)? What kinds of heroic qualities do risk-takers or Olympic athletes need?

A Poem

Write your own poem describing a heroic event.

Here are some examples:

- A player scores the final goal in a championship hockey game.
- An Olympic figure-skater scores perfect 6's.
- A firefighter rescues children from a burning house.

You could begin your poem the way Monica Kulling did:

✎ I hear Wayne Gretsky…
✎ I hear that firefighter…

Responding Activities **123**

Harriet Tubman

Poem by Eloise Greenfield

Harriet Tubman didn't take no stuff
Wasn't scared of nothing neither
Didn't come in this world to be no slave
And wasn't going to stay one either

"Farewell!" she sang to her friends one night
She was mighty sad to leave 'em
But she ran away that dark, hot night
Ran looking for her freedom

She ran to the woods and she ran through the woods
With the slave catchers right behind her
And she kept on going till she got to the North
Where those mean men couldn't find her

Nineteen times she went back South
To get three hundred others
She ran for her freedom nineteen times
To save sisters and brothers
Harriet Tubman didn't take no stuff
Wasn't scared of nothing neither
Didn't come in this world to be no slave
And didn't stay one either

And didn't stay one either

Did You Know ?

Harriet Tubman was born a slave in the southern United States in 1820. She never went to school, and did years of hard labour for her owner. When she heard she was to be sold to another slave owner, she ran away.

Choral Reading

The poem *Harriet Tubman* is a good one to read out loud with a small group of students. That's because

- the words sound like spoken language
- the poem tells an exciting story
- there's lots of repetition

In your group, decide which lines should be spoken by one person, and which could be said by two or more voices together. In your reading, try to express the different emotions Harriet experiences: defiance, sadness, determination, and celebration. When you have had time to practise, present your reading to the class or family members.

Something To Think About!

Harriet has some of the same heroic qualities as Superman, Amelia Earhart, and other heroes in this unit. What are some of these qualities? What makes Harriet a hero? Would you describe her as a super hero? Why or why not?

She escaped to Pennsylvania, a free northern state. But gaining her own freedom wasn't enough. Harriet established a network of Underground Railroad stations from the South all the way into Canada. She returned to the South to free her mother and brothers, and more than 300 other slaves.

Slave owners offered huge rewards for her capture, forcing her to flee to Canada for several years. She died at the age of 93, famous for being the greatest conductor on the Underground Railroad.

The Wreck of the Dispatch

True Story by **JANET LUNN**   Pictures by **JEREMIE WHITE**

"Annie, Annie," cried John, "there must be a shipwreck! I can see a whole long mast heading toward the rocks. Come quick!"

Gathering up her long skirt, Annie came running toward the shore.

"Oh, John, to be sure it's a wreck and small wonder in such a storm. Can there be a single body left alive, do you think? Quick, go fetch Pa while I get the boat in the water."

"Come on Boy." Annie gave a shrill whistle and a big Newfoundland dog came loping around the corner of the house toward her, his fur blowing around him like feathers in the wind.

"It's no day to be looking for survivors from a wreck," said Mr. Harvey when John came bursting into the kitchen with the news, his blue eyes shining with excitement. "No day at all," but all the while he was pulling on his boots. And all the while the six younger Harvey children were dancing around him, clamouring to go along and help with the rescue.

"No! No! No! You young bedlamers! I'll take John because he's twelve now and Annie as she's all but a woman grown and every bit as strong. And with Boy along, we'll do first rate. The rest of you'll be needed here to help your ma make the place ready for the rescued—the Lord willing there be any." Muttering to himself about confounded storms, wrecks, and foolhardy sailors, Mr. Harvey ran down the beach after John.

It was early on a grey Sunday morning in July of the year 1828. The wind was still fierce after the storm that had been raging for days and the sea was high and wild. Gulls were screaming and the smell of dead fish was strong. It wasn't the first such morning one of the Harveys had seen signs of a shipwreck near the shore of their island, for they lived on the Isle aux Morts just off the southwest coast of Newfoundland.

For as long as people had sailed the northern seas, storms had pulled their ships into the treacherous currents and crushed them against the rocks and reefs around that island. Indeed, it was because so many people had died there that the island was called the Isle aux Morts—the Island of the Dead.

"Say your prayers, young 'uns," said Mr. Harvey. They launched the punt into the wild sea and off they went with Mr. Harvey and Annie at the oars, John in the bow as lookout, and the dog in the stern, "for ballast," John told him.

For almost two hours they rowed steadily, their little punt rising high in the crests of the waves and sinking deep into the hollows. There were plenty of signs of the wreck—kegs, benches, trunks, and the ship's name board with DISPATCH written on it—but no sight of the wreck or of people—dead or alive. Then suddenly John shouted, "I see it, I see it!" he cried. "Look over

there!" And there, about a mile out, caught on a large reef was a huge ship, over on its side and heaving and lurching in the heavy sea.

On the same reef there were people. It looked like hundreds, clinging together for comfort and safety, "like great sea birds on their wee rock," said Annie, "the poor drowned folk!"

"Not drowned yet," said her father grimly.

"Ahoy!" he shouted, then, "Ahoy!" shouted all three together with the excited barking of the dog to make their chorus stronger.

At last they were answered by a wave of a cloth and a feeble but happy "Ahoy, ahoy!" from the reef.

They rowed as near as they could to the reef (about a cable's length* from it, John figured) where they could see that there were nearly two hundred people all cheering, crying, and calling them angels.

"Lord's Mercy, however are we going to get two hundred people to safety in this one little punt," said Mr. Harvey, "Two hundred people! Two hundred people," he said over and over again, "Two hundred..."

"We have a rope here," shouted a voice from the reef.

---

*A **cable's length** measures about 180 m.

"And we have another," said John, "we could..."

"We could splice them ropes," said John's dad as though reading John's mind, "and make a line of them here to the shore." He put his hand on the dog's head. "Give an end of your rope to the dog," he shouted to the people on the reef, then he said softly, "In you go, Boy. Swim!"

"Whistle for the boy, here," he shouted, and at once there was a loud whistle from the reef. Then they all watched breathlessly as the big black dog fought his way through the angry sea.

"Good boy! Oh you good boy!" said John and Annie, almost jumping up and down with relief when they saw the dog climb up on the reef. Intently they watched him. Boy waited patiently while a crew member placed a belaying pin*, with a rope knotted round it, into his mouth. The man gave the dog's head a pat and pointed toward the water. Then the dog plunged into the waves again.

"Come home, now, Boy, come along home!" bellowed Mr. Harvey and the dog swam the perilous distance back to the punt.

Working quickly, Mr. Harvey spliced the rope from the wreck to his own rope. John and Annie rowed the boat to shore and anchored the new long rope there. Then Mr. Harvey rigged up a breeches-buoy** to slide along the rope on a pulley. Now the rescue could begin!

One by one, the survivors clambered into the breeches-buoy and rode safely above the breakers to land. Those waiting their turn on the reef, watched and prayed, terrified their turn would never come, that they would die in the ocean as so many of their fellow passengers had already done.

They didn't die, not one of them. The rescue was painfully slow but, by Sunday night, sixty people were brought to shore in the punt. John and Annie rowed several others who were sick or injured home where their mother and the younger children nursed and fed them and found them clothes and a place to sleep.

All that night the rescue went on, all the next day and that night, too, until, by Tuesday morning, all one hundred and sixty-three survivors were safe at the Harvey's home.

---

*A **belaying pin** is a removable pin on the rail of a ship that holds a rope.

A **breeches-buoy is a pair of canvas shorts attached to a life preserver. This buoy slides along a rope on a pulley and can be used to rescue people by moving them from ship to shore.

The survivors—weary, grieved, frightened, and hungry—stayed with the Harveys for ten days while they waited for a ship from St. John's to come for them. The sick were cared for in the small house, the rest camped outside and, somehow, food was found for all of them. The Harveys shared everything they had with their one hundred and sixty-three unexpected guests, then, when they'd gone, settled down to fish and farm as though nothing all that remarkable had happened.

But the governor of Newfoundland thought something remarkable had happened. Two hundred immigrants and a crew of nine bound for Quebec City had set sail from Ireland on the *Dispatch* six weeks earlier. On the Thursday before the Harveys found them, the *Dispatch* had struck the reef. By Sunday morning, forty-six people had drowned. By the Tuesday evening, all the rest had been saved.

The governor sent the Harveys a letter praising them for their heroism and, with the letter, there was a sum of money and a gold medal. The money was soon spent and, in the hundred and seventy years since that time, the letter and the medal have both been lost. But, in Newfoundland, where people love to tell sea stories, one of the stories they love best is about the brave Harvey children and their big, black Newfoundland dog.

◆

How did Isle aux Morts get its name? Do you think ships still get into trouble there? How do you think people are rescued from shipwrecks today?

Understanding the Story

Daring Sea Rescue

- This is a true story, but many of the facts have been changed as the story has been told again and again. What facts do you think might have become exaggerated?

- Who are the heroes in this story? Explain your answer.

- Why do the Harveys ask their dog to swim to the wreck?

- How are the heroes rewarded? Do you think this reward is enough?

Find Out More About...

What's a Newfoundland dog? Research with a partner to find out why these dogs are so amazing!

YOUR TURN TO WRITE

A Letter of Praise

The governor sent the Harveys a letter praising them for their heroism. Think about the rescue and the part each member of the Harvey family played in it. What are the most heroic things each of them did? Now write a letter the governor might have sent to them.

August 15, 1828

Dear Annie and John:

It is with great pleasure that I..........

Yours most gratefully,

Governor of Newfoundland

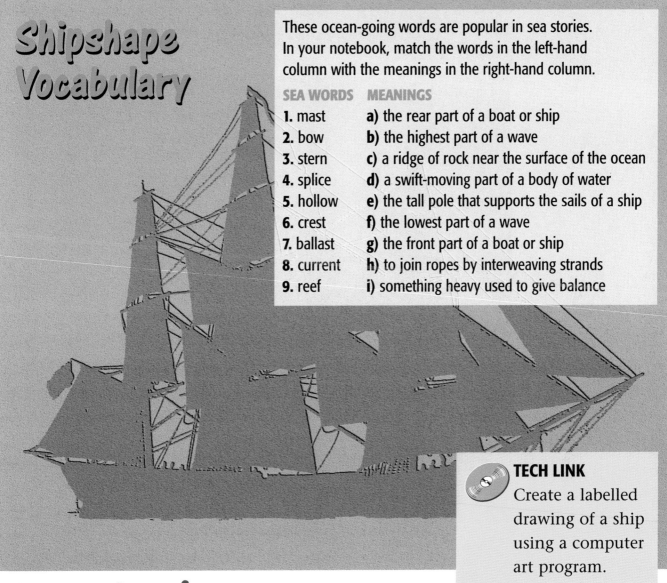

Shipshape Vocabulary

These ocean-going words are popular in sea stories. In your notebook, match the words in the left-hand column with the meanings in the right-hand column.

SEA WORDS	MEANINGS
1. mast	**a)** the rear part of a boat or ship
2. bow	**b)** the highest part of a wave
3. stern	**c)** a ridge of rock near the surface of the ocean
4. splice	**d)** a swift-moving part of a body of water
5. hollow	**e)** the tall pole that supports the sails of a ship
6. crest	**f)** the lowest part of a wave
7. ballast	**g)** the front part of a boat or ship
8. current	**h)** to join ropes by interweaving strands
9. reef	**i)** something heavy used to give balance

TECH LINK
Create a labelled drawing of a ship using a computer art program.

Reader's Theatre

Together with five or six classmates, prepare a dramatic reading of this story. Choose readers for each of these parts: Mr. Harvey, Annie, John, and a couple of survivors from the wreck. These characters will read only their spoken words (look for the speeches in quotation marks).

Also choose one or two group members to be narrators. The narrators will read all the parts between the speeches. It is not necessary to read aloud the words "he said" and "she said."

Take a little time to plan and rehearse your dramatic reading. Decide how you will say your lines to make the story more exciting. When you have rehearsed the story, present it to the class.

BEFORE READING

In your community there may be people less fortunate than you. Take a minute to think about who these people are and how you might help them.

Then read this article to find out how a young girl helps people in her community.

Dwaina Brooks:
Feeding the Homeless

Article by Paula N. Kessler   Pictures by David Bathurst

Every morning on her way to school Dwaina Brooks walked by a line of men and women outside a homeless shelter in her home town. Many of them looked cold and completely worn out. Dwaina noticed that no one ever stopped to talk to these people. They just passed them by.

In school, her class was doing a unit on homelessness. Every week students would call a homeless shelter and talk with someone who was staying there. Dwaina had heard lots of stories. Most people's lives had been going along okay until something had happened. Whether they had lost their jobs or gotten sick, or their family had split up, the result was often the same—they didn't have any money for food or rent, and they had lost their homes.

One day on her way home from school Dwaina stopped to talk to a homeless man. "What do you need?" she asked him.

"I need a job and a home," he said. Dwaina didn't know how she could get him either of those things, so she asked if there was anything else that he needed.

"I'd love a really good meal," the man said. It was at that moment that Dwaina realized how she could help.

She went straight home and told her mom about the man and her class unit on the homeless. Dwaina told her that she wanted to make food for the homeless, and her mother agreed that it was a good idea and that she would be willing to help too.

With Dwaina donating her lunch money (three dollars) to the cause, she and her family came up with sixty dollars to spend. That Friday night, after three days of shopping and planning, cutting coupons, and buying discounted meats, and day-old bread, Dwaina, her mother, and her two sisters got started. They formed an assembly line and began frying chicken, baking cookies, and making sandwiches. They then placed each meal in a box donated by a local baker. By ten that evening, they had made more than one hundred meals, which they drove immediately to the shelter. Many of the people there were asleep, but they were in for a treat the next morning: a real home-cooked meal.

After that, Dwaina was hooked on helping the homeless. To subsidize the cost of the food, she and her family sought help and donations from bakeries and grocery stores. Then, nearly every Friday night for an entire year, Dwaina, her mother, and her sisters made about one hundred meals for the shelter. But Dwaina wanted to make more meals. The only way to do this, however, was to get more help, so Dwaina talked to her class at school. She told her classmates what her mother and sisters had been doing over the past year.

The following Friday, twenty-three kids from Dwaina's class came over to her house, each with some type of food to contribute. By midnight they'd prepared more than three hundred meals, enough for everyone in the shelter to have one.

Dwaina Brooks, now fourteen, has organized thousands of meals for the homeless. She hopes to become a doctor and open her own clinic someday, but she thinks it's crazy to wait until then to start caring for others.

"Each of us should have some kind of concern in our hearts for other people," Dwaina says. "And we owe it, too. There isn't a one of us who hasn't been helped by someone else. You should always be ready to give back what people have given to you." ◆

FOLLOW UP

What makes Dwaina a hero? Compare her heroism to that of another hero in this unit.

Personal Response

Sometimes you hear people say, "It's such a big problem. There's nothing one person can do about it."

Have you seen homeless people in your community or a nearby city? Why do you think they are homeless? What do you think can be done to help them? Discuss your thoughts, ideas, and solutions with a partner.

Take Action!

Pick a group of people less fortunate than you and do something to help them. You can help older adults in your neighbourhood with their shopping, bring flowers to the sick, or, like Dwaina, make food for a homeless shelter. Your help and support will be greatly appreciated and will make you feel really good.

TIP Discuss your plans with your parents or guardians.

Understanding the Article

Food For Thought

• What did Dwaina's class at school do to try and understand the problem of homelessness?

• How did Dwaina decide what she personally could do to help the homeless?

• Why did she decide it was important to help other people?

• Did she prove that one person can do something about a big problem? Explain your answer.

Media Link

Disasters in the News

Long ago, victims of floods, earthquakes, or other disasters had to rely on themselves and their neighbours for help. Now, people around the world hear the news and send help immediately. Here are some photos of recent disasters in Canada. People across the country sent money, food, blankets, clothing, electric generators—whatever was needed to help the people who were suffering. Collect articles or other photos like these and find out how some people lend a hand.

Next time you hear of a disaster, try organizing your class to help the victims. You *can* make a difference!

Something To Think About!

What kind of hero is Dwaina? She didn't slay a monster, and she knew she wouldn't receive a reward. She helped others with no thought for herself. This is called "altruism." Make a class list of people you know who act in altruistic ways to help less fortunate people.

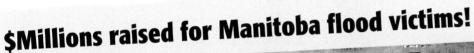

$Millions raised for Manitoba flood victims!

In May 1997, thousands of people were forced from their homes when the Red River flooded.

Thousands send blankets; electric generators to Ottawa, Montréal.

Volunteers help victims of ice storms

In January 1998, a severe ice storm left people in the Ottawa valley, through to Montréal, without electricity.

The First of Many Steps

Profile by
LESLIE GARRETT

Map by
BILL SUDDICK

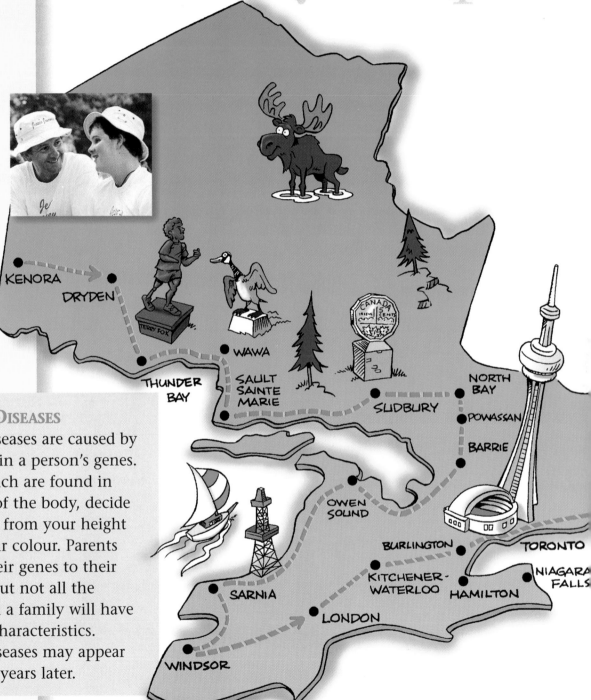

GENETIC DISEASES

Genetic diseases are caused by a problem in a person's genes. Genes, which are found in every cell of the body, decide everything from your height to your hair colour. Parents pass on their genes to their children, but not all the children in a family will have the same characteristics. Genetic diseases may appear at birth or years later.

Jesse Davidson knows first-hand the difficulties and pain that genetic diseases cause. Jesse has Duchenne muscular dystrophy—a disease that attacks the muscles of boys. Over a number of years, the muscles weaken and cannot support the body.

On April 10, 1994, Jesse Davidson and his father, John, went out to a local restaurant in their home town of London, Ontario, to celebrate Jesse's fourteenth birthday. Jesse expected a quiet night out, but John had something very important he wanted to discuss.

"Are you crazy?" Jesse's dark eyes opened wide when his dad outlined his plan for the two of them to cross Ontario together— John on foot, Jesse in his wheelchair. They would raise money and awareness to help those with genetic diseases.

"After all," John reminded his son, "look what Terry Fox and his Marathon of Hope did for cancer research."

"What about school?" asked Jesse. "I'll have to be away for a long time." And, he asked, where would they get the funding to support them? Where would they get supplies? Jesse also knew that such a journey would be very hard work.

John Davidson wasn't surprised at his son's reluctance. Jesse, a cautious, organized kid, liked to think things through. But Jesse soon became excited about the idea. It made him happy to realize that he would be raising money for a good cause, and helping others like himself. "I didn't want to be a role model," Jesse says now. "I just wanted to be someone who set a goal, and met it."

John, Jesse, and his mother Sherene, set their financial goal at $1 million. The money would be donated to the Foundation for Gene and Cell Therapy. Then they got to work planning "Jesse's Journey," as it was named. They found sponsors and raised funds. They recruited volunteers to help drive the motor home that would follow John and Jesse. They also hired two assistants. Tricia Federkow would tend to John and Jesse's muscle aches and blisters and would also arrange food and shelter. Sean Bagshaw would look after Jesse's special physical needs. People with muscular dystrophy tire extremely easily, and everyone knew the trip would be particularly hard on Jesse.

JESSE'S JOURNEY BEGINS

Jesse's Journey began on a cold, drizzly day in May 1995, at the border of Ontario and Manitoba. There were only a few supporters to send them off. The roads were hilly and the summer quickly became one of the hottest in years.

"It was repetitive," says Jesse. "There were so many hills that were exhausting."

Jesse had to be sure to get lots of rest. John, at forty-nine years old, was in good shape. But the 30 km a day of walking took its toll on him as well. Still, every day they got up, and pushed on. Behind them came the motor home carrying the assistants, volunteers, and all their supplies.

Outside Thunder Bay, John and Jesse stopped at the monument to Terry Fox, whose Marathon of Hope inspired people around the world. Jesse gazed up at the statue, gathering strength from the runner's words: "Dreams are made if people only try," he read. "I believe in miracles. I have to, because somewhere the hurting must stop."

The two picked up steam. They had already travelled more than 500 km on their journey and people were starting to take notice.

Just outside of Wawa, a woman approached Jesse and asked him to name a ten-day-old colt for her. Her thirteen-year-old daughter was supposed to name it, but she hadn't lived long enough. She had died of a genetic disease. Jesse went to her farm and named the young horse "Snowy," for the white blaze on its face.

HALFWAY POINT

It was a beautiful hot, sunny day when they arrived in Powassan. They had put 1652 km behind them and had roughly the same distance to go. "Jessie's Journey: Halfway Point" read the huge banner stretching across the road. John began to jog, and he and Jesse burst through the banner—or tried to.

Instead of ripping, as planned, the banner wrapped itself around the excited pair. Laughing, they untangled themselves, and Jesse grinned and waved at the crowd. The streets were filled with cheering people offering words of encouragement. Jesse was becoming a celebrity, and he happily signed small Canadian flags for the boys and girls who gathered around him.

By the time John and Jesse entered southwestern Ontario, their journey was gaining more attention. They were met by bigger crowds, they were collecting more money, and they were nearing their home town of London.

On August 21, the day they'd been dreaming about arrived. Three months and 2635 km later, the two arrived to a thunderous welcome. Thousands of people lined the streets to offer warm wishes and cold hard cash to their home town heroes. On that one day, Londoners donated more than $75 000 to research into genetic diseases. To add to the wonderful day, the mayor announced that a local park would be named Jesse Davidson Park.

ALMOST THERE!

Back on the road again, John and Jesse saw Jesse's grandparents in Woodstock, and then travelled on to the big city of Toronto. They spent a day doing television and newspaper interviews, telling people about their journey and what they hoped to achieve.

Jesse also enjoyed a visit to the Hockey Hall of Fame, where hockey legend Darryl Sittler presented him with a Maple Leafs sweater. But, being a true baseball fan, his greatest thrill was to be invited onto the field at the SkyDome to wave to the fans of the Blue Jays—and of Jesse Davidson. The next day they were on the highway early, but they knew the end was near.

On September 20, John and Jesse reached Ottawa. More than 3300 km and four months had passed. Jesse's Journey had raised $800 000, and their goal was within reach. Despite the drizzle, the mood was festive, and Jesse and John were thrilled when Prime Minister Jean Chrétien met them on Parliament Hill. Afterwards, people cheered them along the last few kilometres of their long journey.

Finally, Jesse and John approached the finish line on the Québec side of the Alexandra Bridge. Jesse burst through the banner, and suddenly all their hard work, aching muscles, long days and blisters were worth it. "We did it," said Jesse quietly, a smile lighting up his face.

FOLLOW UP

Three months later, with donations still coming in, Jesse's Journey reached its goal of $1 million for gene and cell research. May 20, the day the journey began, has become a day of hope for families and friends of those with genetic diseases.

For Jesse, the journey was more than a chance to raise money for a very worthy cause. "I found out what I could do, what my abilities were," he says. "I found out that if I had a goal and I tried, at least I'd feel satisfied with what I did."

In September 1996, Jesse and his father were awarded their province's highest honour—the Order of Ontario. ◗

Did you predict what *The First of Many Steps* would be about, or did the article surprise you? What did you like best about Jesse's story?

Something To Think About

Jesse says, "I just wanted to be someone who set a goal, and met it." Do you have a personal goal you would like to meet? Reaching a goal takes many small steps. Write down the first two steps you will take to help you achieve your goal.

Understanding the Article

A Long Way Home

- Why was Jesse reluctant at first to set out on a long journey? How would you have reacted in Jesse's place?

- What goals did this father-and-son team set for themselves? What helped them reach those goals?

- What do you think Jesse liked most about the trip? What do you think he liked least? Explain your answers.

- How did Jesse's life change as a result of his achievement? How did he change the lives of others?

Design a Certificate

Design a certificate or plaque to honour Jesse and his father. Make some decisions about what will be on it.

Will you quote some of Jesse's own words? Will you use illustrations or photos? Will you include a map of his journey? Share your work with others, explaining what it represents.

Find Out More About...

Terry Fox had a goal: to run across Canada and raise money for cancer research. Today, people still get together to run and raise money in his memory.

Find out about Terry's dream, the obstacles he faced, and the success he had. Use library or Internet resources to help you. Then write a paragraph explaining why Terry Fox is a hero to so many people.

MORE GOOD READING

HEROES Old and New

🍁 **Atalanta: The Fastest Runner in the World**
by Priscilla Galloway
Young Atalanta wants to run and hunt, and her speed and strength will take her a long way. Finally, though, the goddess Artemis may determine her destiny! (a Greek myth)

🍁 **Super Kids**
by Leslie Garrett
In these inspiring stories, kids perform daring and selfless deeds. Just two examples: Brad, who stopped a runaway car with three small children inside; and Amelia, who saved her grandmother's life. (true stories)

The Wave of the Sea-Wolf
by David Wisniewski
The intelligent and brave Kchokeen saves her people, with the help of the Sea-Wolf, a water spirit. (a Tlingit legend)

🍁 **Animal Heroes**
by Kathleen Bradford
In these amazing tales the heroes are animals. Many are faithful dogs that rescue people, but there's also Cali the Guard Cat, and others. (true stories)

Make a Magazine

Wild, Wild Horses

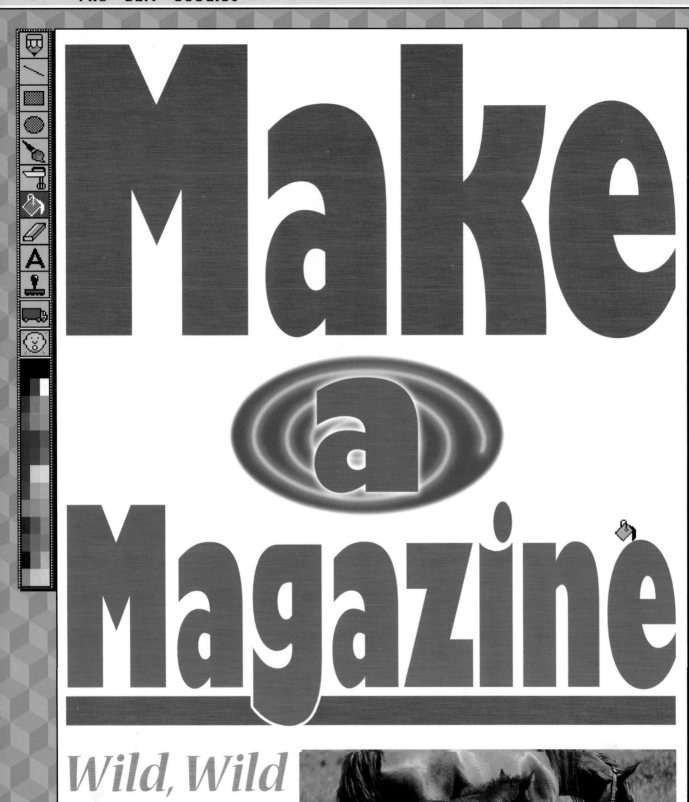

Take The Great Canadian Nutrition Challenge

kidsworld
MAGAZINE
Spring 1998

Volume 6, Issue 2

May 1998   The Discovery Magazine for Kids $2.95

OWL

Bikers
Grind Gears,
Saucers
Fly High,
+ Circles
Drop By

This
**Helmet
Head**
Has Its
Eye
on
You

Get
Face to Face
with the
**World's
Deadliest
Bird!**

cowary

OWL

Cricket

$3.95 ($5.95 in U.S.)
may 1998
for ages 9 and up

New Moon
The Magazine for Girls and Their Dreams
MAY · JUNE 1998 · USA $5.50 · CAN $7.50

WEIRD MASCOTS ★ COOL SPORTS SLANG ★ STANLEY CUP CRAZY

U.S.A. $2.95 Canada $3.95
May 1998

Sports Illustrated
FOR
KIDS

DAVID ROBINSON AND
TIM DUNCAN OF THE
SAN ANTONIO SPURS

**YIPPIE!
YAHOOP!**

VISIT OUR WEBSITE AT WWW.SIKIDS.COM

YES Mag
Canada's Science Magazine For Kids

Forensic
Science

BEFORE READING

In this selection, you'll tour the offices of *Kaleidoscope,* an imaginary magazine for kids. Read on to find out how each staff member makes the magazine happen!

Let's Tour
Kaleidoscope

Information by Catherine Rondina

Comic Strip by Steve Attoe

Hi! Welcome to *Kaleidoscope,* a magazine for kids. I'm Matt, and I'm doing a project on how to put a magazine together. Come along while I talk to the people who know all about it!

Publisher–Lotta Cents

Editor–Harvey Headhoncho

Managing Editor–Sasha Schedule

Kid Panel– The Just-Ask-Us Gang

Associate Editor– Malva Main-Idea

Copy Editor– Harland Hawkeye

Fact Checker– Fiona For-Sure

Features Department

Sports Editor– Olivia Olympia

Games Editor–Chris Crossword

Music Editor– Ruth Rocker

TV & Movie Editor– Ricki Remote

Services Department

Art Department

Photo Editor– Carmen Camera

Art Director–Deepak Design

Printing Plant

Circulation Department

Oh, here's Ricki Remote! You have a great job.

Right, Matt—TV and movie editor! I have to know what TV shows and movies kids are watching, so I get to research all the new and exciting shows.

Our Kid Panel is really helpful here. When I have the information I need, I write a short article. Sometimes I even hire photographers.

All the other service editors do the same for their own topics.

Hello, Deepak Design. Love your computer!

Hi, Matt. Yes, I couldn't do a thing without my computer. It helps me to give *Kaleidoscope* that special look.

But first, I assign artists to draw illustrations, and then approve the photos the photo editor selects.

Then every page of the magazine has to be laid out so that text, photos, and drawings all work together.

The idea is to attract the readers' attention with strong colours and bold type.

After a lot of work— ABRACADABRA!— the magazine is finished.

Kaleidoscope is printed and bound at the printing plant. Then the copies are ready for distribution. The Circulation Department makes sure magazines are shipped to subscribers and newsstands around the country.

So now we both know how to make a magazine!

FOLLOW UP

If you worked for a kids' magazine, which job would you like to have? Explain why.

Join the Kid Panel

You've just joined the Just-Ask-Us Gang! Get together with five or six classmates and brainstorm ideas for this month's issue of *Kaleidoscope*. It's a general-interest magazine, so you can choose any topics you like. Here are a few hints:

- Remember the age and interests of the magazine's readers.
- Include what's new and exciting in sports, music, and entertainment.
- Decide which topics should be feature articles (longer) and which should be short articles.

Understanding the Article

Matt's Magazine Project

While touring *Kaleidoscope* Matt made lots of notes. Then, before writing up his project, he made an outline. Your job is to help Matt fill in his outline. In your notebook, write a sentence or two telling what each staff member does to help put the magazine together.

A: Planning the next issue of *Kaleidoscope*

a) Editor

b) Managing Editor

c) Kid Panel

B: Writing the articles

a) Associate Editor

b) Service Editors

C: Creating the "look" of the magazine

a) Photo Editor

b) Art Director

D: Doing the final polishing

a) Fact Checker

b) Copy Editor

Make a Table of Contents

Here's your chance to create the ultimate magazine! In your group, choose at least ten ideas you had in "Join the Kid Panel." For each idea, make up a catchy title. Develop titles for the standing columns, too. (For examples, see page 150.)

Now, record your ideas and titles in a table of contents for your magazine. Include the titles of feature and short articles, and standing columns, and the month your magazine will be published.

- article about how to set up an aquarium
- title: Tropical Dreamfish

IMAGINE!

Design a cover for the next issue of *Kaleidoscope*.

(For examples, see page 150.)

Did You Know ?

A copy editor or proofreader will use the following marks when editing text.

Copy Editor's Marks

Symbol	Meaning	Example
⌃	insert comma	Fiona checks dates, places, names...
⌒	cut letter	Deepak uses a computer.
⋏#	add space between words	New and exciting shows...
≡ cap	make this a capital letter	I asked Lotta cents. cap
⌐	indent paragraph	I'm Matt, and I'm doing a...

TIP Try using these marks when you're correcting your own work!

**BEFORE
READING**

Going Buggy in the Trees (page 54) first appeared as a feature article in a real kids' magazine, called *Wild.* Read on to find out how the *Wild* magazine team made it happen.

Article by
Susan Hughes

"Going Buggy" at WILD

The *Wild* Team

Martin McLennan,
Photo Editor

Kendra Toby,
Associate Editor

Martin Silverstone,
Editor

Douglas Cowell,
Writer-Photographer

Where Do Magazines Get Story Ideas?

Martin Silverstone, Kendra Toby, and Martin McLennan all meet. They're scratching their heads, trying to figure out next year's issues. One of the ideas to consider is an e-mail message from Douglas Cowell—a writer who's also a photographer. He wants to write a story about treetop insect research in British Columbia. Everyone loves the idea! Quickly they add one more feature article to their chart. Possible title: "Going Buggy!"

"Can we publish this in the February issue?" Martin Silverstone asks Kendra.

"I'll give it my best shot," she replies.

Time to Call in the Writer

Kendra reaches writer-photographer Douglas Cowell on the phone. "I'm from *Wild*. We like your story idea," she says.

"Great!" says Douglas. "When's my deadline?"

"Six weeks from now," she replies. "And another thing. We'd like you to take a kid along for the ride."

"Good suggestion. I know a kid who'd love an adventure like this."

"Okay. I'm looking forward to reading your story. And seeing some exciting pictures!" Kendra signs off.

Don't Forget the Tape Recorder!

Douglas makes a few phone calls. He sets up a visit to the research station at Rocky Point. Then he arranges for his young friend Faron to come along.

They have a great day. Douglas knows *Wild* wants action shots of Faron climbing up to the treetop station, so he takes many photos. He also mutters quite a lot.

"Why are you talking to yourself?" asks Faron, when they reach the top.

"Bad habit!" claims Douglas, winking. "Actually, I have a miniature tape recorder in my pocket. I'm recording everything I see and do. Plus, I plan to interview the scientists up here. And I'm recording your every word."

"Wow!" says Faron. "I'd better watch out!"

Beating the Blank Paper Blues

The next day, Douglas takes his photos in to be developed. When he gets them back, he labels them and weeds out the poor ones. Then he listens to his tapes and takes notes from them.

A few days later, he sits down with his notes, photos, and tapes. "I hate a blank piece of paper," he groans. "I'd better make one of my trusty webs."

Pencil in hand, he asks himself, "What is this article about?" He writes down some main ideas, such as *Insects*. Then he makes a web of ideas around each idea.

Try the First-Person Voice...

Douglas is feeling better. He's made an outline of the article on his computer. Now he's ready to begin the real writing!

First, he works on a rough draft.

He wants to tell an exciting story from beginning to end. Part way through he calls Faron. "Would you mind if I told this story in your voice?" he asks.

"You mean, 'My name is Faron Nicholas. I'm in grade seven in Victoria.' That kind of thing?"

"That's right. I think *Wild's* readers would enjoy it more."

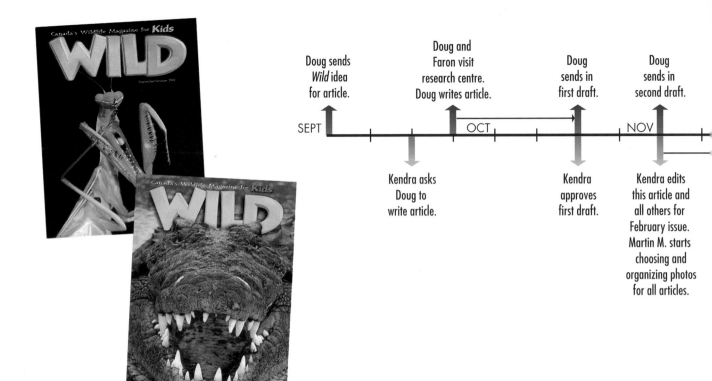

Doug sends *Wild* idea for article.

Doug and Faron visit research centre. Doug writes article.

Doug sends in first draft.

Doug sends in second draft.

SEPT   OCT   NOV

Kendra asks Doug to write article.

Kendra approves first draft.

Kendra edits this article and all others for February issue. Martin M. starts choosing and organizing photos for all articles.

"It's fine with me," Faron says. "As long as I don't have to write the article!"

"Great. I'll be checking some facts with you, too." Douglas hangs up and returns to the computer.

Can't Miss That Deadline

Douglas has his second draft ready, just in time. He does a word count and prints out the article. Now he lets Faron read it.

"I like it," Faron declares. "But it sure needs photos!"

"Don't worry," Douglas reassures him. "*Wild* will make the published article look terrific."

Douglas does one last check of his spelling and grammar. The final version is ready to go to Kendra by courier.

Kendra e-mails him as soon as his package arrives. "Congratulations! You've met your deadline!"

Caution: Editor at Work

Kendra passes the photos on to Martin McLennan. Then she reads Doug's article, making sure the story flows. She wants her readers to feel that they could have been there—right up in the trees with Faron.

"Hey, this guy is a good writer," she mutters to herself. "His article doesn't need any corrections. I'll just have to shorten it a little."

Kendra adds a pronunciation guide for the word "carabiner," and a definition for "extirpated." Then she moves on to fact-checking. If she can't find the information she needs, she can always phone a bug expert. Finally, she asks the freelance copy editor to do a last check for spelling and grammar mistakes.

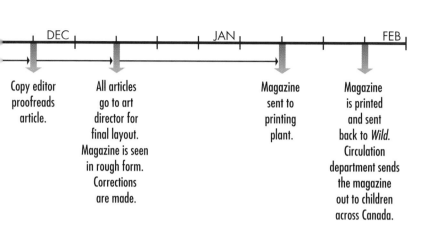

Timeline:

DEC | JAN | FEB

Copy editor proofreads article.

All articles go to art director for final layout. Magazine is seen in rough form. Corrections are made.

Magazine sent to printing plant.

Magazine is printed and sent back to *Wild*. Circulation department sends the magazine out to children across Canada.

What's a Magazine Without Pictures?

Martin, the photo editor, starts thinking about the "look" of the article, and the photos he's going to use. "A photo has to be clear and sharp," he always says. "It should have strong colour contrasts, too."

He selects the best of Douglas's photos. For the opening shot, he picks the photo of Faron in his climbing harness. It's exciting and draws the reader in. Also, it's vertical, and emphasizes the great height of those trees!

He chooses about ten photos which help tell the story.

Next, he sends a list of bugs to a specialist in insect photography. He receives a package of close-up bug shots, all accurately labelled.

Finally, he does thumbnail sketches (tiny drawings) of each page of the article. The sketches show where the photos and text will go.

On to the Next Issue!

All of the articles for the February issue are ready. Kendra sends them off to the printing house. Soon the magazine is published, in full colour.

"Wow," says Kendra. "This is our best issue ever!" She shows it off to everybody in the office. Then she throws it in a drawer. *Going Buggy in the Trees* will soon be in the hands of kids like you—the magazine's readers. But she and the other staff members are already hard at work on the next issue of *Wild!* ⬡

With a partner, discuss how *Wild* and *Kaleidoscope* magazines are the same, and how they are different.

Understanding the Article

Wild for Magazines

- Why do you think the *Wild* editors want Faron to go along on the expedition into the treetops? How does Faron help Douglas Cowell?

- What process does Cowell use as he writes? How is the way Cowell writes the same, or different, from the way you write?

- Which job at the magazine would you like to have? Why?

- Why is it important for all the people at the magazine to work together like a team?

Viewing — Be a Photo Editor

You have been sent a batch of photos for an article on Dall's sheep called "Wild and Woolly." Choose the photo you would use for each of these purposes:

- the first photo in the article, "Wild and Woolly"
- a photo that shows how sure-footed Dall's sheep are
- a photo that shows the sheep's habitat
- a photo that brings readers face-to-face with a sheep

Be ready to explain your choices to the art director!

Notes into Paragraphs

Writers make notes when they do research and when they interview somebody. At right are one writer's point-form notes on Dall's sheep, for an article in *Wild* magazine. Each heading is a new topic.

When the writer was ready to write the article, she turned her notes into paragraphs. Each topic starts a new paragraph. For example:

> Dall's sheep are sure-footed animals that live high in the mountain valleys of northern British Columbia. They can also be found in the Yukon and Alaska.

Now turn the other two topics into paragraphs. You've just written a three-paragraph report!

habitat
- sure-footed animals can climb
- live in mountain valleys in northern BC
- also found in Yukon and Alaska

birth
- lambs born in May
- weigh about 4 kg
- able to trot around after a week

migration
- herds migrate every year
- climb 2000 m to new grazing ground
- oldest ram leads the herd

IMAGINE!
Create your own magazine, with the help of classmates. Give it a catchy name, then write and illustrate the articles.